**DO NOT REMOVE
CARDS FROM POCKET**

William Paul Steele

STAY HOME AND STAR!

A Step-by-Step Guide to Starting Your
Regional Acting Career
in
commercials... industrials... theatre...
movies... print modeling...
newscasting... radio and
television reporting

HEINEMANN
Portsmouth
New Hampshire

HEINEMANN EDUCATIONAL BOOKS, INC.
361 Hanover Street   Portsmouth, NH 03801–3959
Offices and agents throughout the world

Library of Congress Cataloging-in-Publication Data

Steele, William Paul.
    Stay home and star! : a step-by-step guide to starting
your regional acting career / William Paul Steele.
        p.   cm.
    ISBN 0-435-08603-0
    1. Acting—Vocational guidance.   I. Title.
PN2055.S75   1992
792'.028'02373—dc20   91-14981
                                                      CIP

Design by Wladislaw Finne
Printed in the United States of America
92 93 94 95 96 10 9 8 7 6 5 4 3 2 1

Contents

Preface **vii**

Acknowledgments **xi**

Chapter One
Preparation, the Unions, and Reality **1**

Chapter Two
Getting Ready for Commercials **11**

Chapter Three
Looking for Work in Commercials **33**

Chapter Four
Working in Commercials **49**

Chapter Five
Corporate and Educational Markets **73**

Chapter Six
Theatre and Movies **103**

Chapter Seven
Commercial and Corporate Print **115**

Chapter Eight
Radio and Television News, Weather, and Sports   **129**

Appendix A
The Major Actors' Unions   **143**

Appendix B
Recommended Practical Reading   **149**

Appendix C
How to Get a Wireless Earprompter   **153**

℘reface

"Sometimes it's better to be a big fish in a small pond."

You want to be a professional actor but don't know where or how to begin. Maybe you've had some training and maybe you haven't, but you've imagined yourself in plays, movies, and commercials, or on the pages of magazines. And you've been told that your chances are minimal, that there's tremendous competition, that maybe you'll have to move to New York or Hollywood, and that it may take years to succeed.

If you're like most of the prospective actors I know and teach, the above is probably true. Professional acting is a *business*, and the business of acting is difficult to penetrate, anywhere. But don't be misled, because the best and easiest place to start an acting career is in a small or midsize city. And it just may be the best place to stay.

Certainly there are many opportunities for actors in New York and Hollywood, but there are thousands of out-of-work actors there, too. And it takes too much time to get started there. It's much better to begin as a regional actor where things are simpler and where you don't have to join a union right away to qualify for work.

This book will tell you where to find acting jobs in a small or midsize (or larger) city and will give you a step-by-step strategy for breaking into the world of the working actor. And while it's addressed directly to the beginner, it will also provide valuable insights to those New York and Hollywood actors who want to market themselves on a smaller but not necessarily less rewarding scale—actors who may already be union members with national credits but who lack experience selling themselves regionally.

Almost every city in the United States has opportunities for actors in radio and television commercials, corporate and educational video and films, theatre, movies, and print modeling. There are also jobs for actors who want to segue into local radio and television news, weather, and sports. All of these employment markets are constantly crying for new faces and voices.

It's a myth that you need matinee idol looks or a whiskey voice to succeed. Quite the contrary. There's potential work out there for just about everyone—with or without acting experience. You just need to know how to find it. And once you find it you need to know how to get that first job, and the next, and the next.

In spite of regional (and sometimes national) economic ups and downs, there's always plenty of opportunity for the local and regional actor. National advertisers frequently target commercials at specific regional, ethnic, and special-interest markets. Filmmakers are turning to regional locations more frequently, often using entire towns—and lots of the people who live there—in scenes. Television shows and miniseries are taped all over the country. The theatre, although constantly struggling for financial stability, continues to flourish at the grassroots. Corporate television is *everywhere*, and it's here to stay. Once you know where to look, you'll be surprised at the opportunities right there in your own home town.

This book is structured to lead you to that work with a minimum of roadblocks and with no pie-in-the-sky promises. Each of the following chapters covers a specific acting category and gives you proven, practical advice for success.

And when and if you're ready to join a union or branch out to New York or Hollywood, where the rules of the game

change, Appendix B suggests plenty of reading to help you
fit in.

But remember, sometimes it *is* better to be a big fish in a
small pond.

You've heard that saying before; so have I. But when a
lighting technician on a commercial shoot several years ago
brought it into our conversation, it really hit home.

I was in New York, cast as the spokesperson for a couple
of Citibank television commercials, finally working in the Big
Apple after months of auditions with seemingly endless call-
backs. It was exciting and fulfilling, the culmination of lots of
pavement pounding, an effort supported by a good and
faithful New York City agent who was getting me in all the
right doors. I had arrived!

I took this foray into the "big time" after developing a successful regional acting career in which I performed in
hundreds of radio and television commercials, appeared in
scores of corporate films and videos, acted in summer stock,
and even had speaking roles in a couple of movies—all
within easy commuting distance of my home, just outside
Portland, Maine. I had joined the Screen Actors Guild (SAG)
and the American Federation of Radio and Television Artists
(AFTRA) by then, and the lure of New York was seductive,
the challenges intoxicating. I felt ready. I had to give it a try.

But the reality was a letdown. Although I successfully com-
peted for a few acting jobs in addition to the Citibank spots
and had spent my childhood in New York City, I wasn't sure
I was ready for the quality of life actors who live there have
to endure. I soon realized that my regional career was the
one I should nurture and continue to develop. And what was
to stop me from occasionally farming the fields of New York
from afar? Nothing.

So that's what I did and still do. Perhaps the same strategy
will work for you: *stay home and star*!

Acknowledgments

This text would not have been produced without the invaluable aid of my wife Eleanor, who suggested I write it in the first place; my literary agent, Ray Powers of the Marje Fields/Rita Scott Agency, for encouragement and extensive practical input; Herm Schwenk, for helping me start my regional acting career; Maggie Trichon, for everything she taught me about the Boston acting/print game; Tersh Raybold, Collins Dickenson, Jim Hanna, Ann Whalen, Jerry Engleson, Ross Bertran, Cole Taminnen, Dave Briggs, Bob Boyd, Mike Welber, John McKeith, Everett Foster, Eric Jorgenson, Rocky Lane, Bob Feldman, Linda Holt, Lynn Kippax, Paul Argerow, Don Moore, Janet Green, Elizabeth Clarke, and Lynn McCann, who submitted to interviews, whether they knew it or not; Laura Butterworth, of the Portland Models Group, for assisting me with "local" print and film information; Alec Diamon and Jeff Marks, for their input on the radio and television news chapter; Lisa Barnett, of Heinemann Educational Books, for her many suggestions in the editorial process of publishing this book; Addy Harkavy; and the University of Southern Maine College of Arts and Sciences Faculty Development Fund, for travel assistance.

Chapter

Preparation, the Unions, and Reality

Having an impressive list of acting instructors on your résumé is unquestionably important in the national acting arenas, but is it really necessary in the smaller markets? *Of course it is*, particularly if you want to demonstrate that you are a serious, professional actor seeking acting work on an ongoing basis. It's no secret that most successful professionals in this field never stop trying to improve their skills.

In general, producers and directors of local and regional commercials, corporate videos and films, theatre, print advertisements, and even theatrical films are *somewhat* more trusting and a bit more willing to give the inexperienced person a chance, if he or she looks and sounds right. But without experience, you need to feel prepared enough to demonstrate the confidence that inspires others. If you have no acting, public speaking, or other performance background, some classes will be of great benefit, and you can list them on your resume.

Generic classes you might consider taking at the outset include acting scenework, acting for the camera, voice and diction for the actor, commercial acting techniques, auditioning techniques for theatre and film, corporate narration techniques, and self-promotion for the actor. Obviously you may not need all these courses, and you certainly won't be able to take them all at the same time, but you can chip away at them as the need arises and as time—and your bankbook—permit.

Certainly many of you reading this are students in or graduates of theatre and film programs in colleges and universities. If so, you have direct access to or have already taken many of the above courses. If you're thinking about entering this field without this obvious leg up you'll have to do some scrambling.

Major cities such as Boston, Atlanta, Seattle, or Houston have many schools that offer professional acting courses. If you live in or near one of these or similar cities, call or write the Screen Actors Guild or Actors' Equity Association branch near you (*see Appendix A*) and ask for the names of good, *legitimate* acting schools, classes, and workshops. Enroll in as many as you have time and money for, and get busy. The more time you spend in front of a group, camera, or microphone, be it time at work or time in class, the more you will build your skills and gain self-confidence.

But be warned! There are lots of scam artists out there just waiting to prey on susceptible people dreaming about an acting career. You want to take classes from the best, people who know what they're doing. Don't rely on slick advertisements to choose your instructors. Rely on professional recommendations instead.

An important side-benefit of taking legitimate, professional classes is that the instructors tend to know lots of people in the business and can act as a reference for you.

Even outside the major cities, there are bound to be traditional acting or other performance courses available to you. Check with the professional theatres in your area to see whether they offer specialized acting or voice classes. Do you live near a college or university that has a theatre department? This can be a wonderful resource for both curriculum and practical suggestions! If taking college courses during the day is impossible, find out whether acting and speech courses are offered at night or on a noncredit basis. Many colleges (especially community ones) and universities are actively seeking nontraditional students in the face of shrinking full-time student enrollments.

And while you're at it, if you are enrolled in a college

course or two, go out for those college theatre productions, try to get cast in a student film, or volunteer your time to the campus radio and TV stations. The valuable experience you'll gain will be well worth the time and effort, and these experiences will help you flesh out your résumé.

Another way to get practice and training is to join (if you haven't already) your local community theatre group. Try out for every play that has a role you think is even remotely right for your type. You'll get priceless experience and lots of feedback. And remember this: producers and directors go to community theatre too, so you may be seen by some people who count.

You may find it comforting to know that most career actors never stop taking classes to improve their line-reading techniques, their vocal quality, and their ability to move. These skills are their bread and butter, and it makes good financial sense to invest in maintaining those skills. They think of it as continuing education and operate under the quite accurate theory that they can always get better.

In conjunction with any and all of the above training avenues, you must *practice reading out loud*. Do it whenever you can—as often as you can—throughout your career. When you have your first audition—be it for a TV commercial, corporate narration, or theatrical role—you'll understand why.

When you read out loud, your objective is to learn several valuable skills vital to your future success. You must learn to read smoothly and without hesitation, to use vocal variety, to develop eye contact, to manipulate tempo, and to vary energy levels. A mirror and an audio tape recorder are invaluable aids for your practice sessions.

The ability to *read smoothly and without hesitation* is essential, particularly in the commercial and corporate arenas. The simple truth is that no one will cast you for a speaking part without watching you and hearing you read. They'll want evidence of your ability to read smoothly under the stress of scrutiny. Unless you've done it plenty of times before, that scrutiny can be inhibiting. Practice gives you not only the skill, but also the confidence to read well in front of strangers when a job is on the line.

Plan to read out loud for at least fifteen minutes a day, every day. Begin without a mirror or tape recorder, and read anything you can get your hands on: the newspaper, magazine articles, books, whatever. Stay away from actual commercial copy and don't worry about eye contact until you can read plain prose smoothly and with little effort. This may take some time, but don't let that stop you.

When you're comfortable with your ability to read smoothly, it's time to add *eye contact*. What you want to do here is look your listener in the eye as much as possible while you're reading without making mistakes. Practice by using something to look at that won't distract you. A spot on an empty wall is fine for this purpose. Scan each sentence as you read and try to look at the wall about halfway through. This will probably be difficult at first, but it won't take long to get the hang of it. When the wall gives you no trouble, practice in front of a mirror so you can see how you look and how you alter your body movements to fit the material.

Once you are proficient at reading out loud, it's time to work on *vocal variety* in terms of reading speed, volume, and pitch. Read aloud at several speeds so you become as comfortable speaking slowly or rapidly as you are speaking at a normal rate. Do the same with volume. Use your tape recorder here to track your progress.

Pitch is somewhat more complicated. Monotony is what you'll try to avoid. Varying pitch levels and emphasizing key words helps you keep what you're reading interesting. Very few people are born with true monotone voices. Those of us who speak monotonously do so because we lack vocal expression or are unwilling to learn to speak more expressively. The actor, no matter at what professional level, must be physically and vocally expressive. (See Appendix B for a list of suggested readings on voice and diction.)

When you can read smoothly with eye contact and variety, you can begin using advertisements and corporate brochures. You'll find plenty in magazines and newspapers and in the lobbies of major businesses, such as banks and insurance companies. Try to read them with lots of positive energy. Unless they're mood pieces, such as antidrug spots or similar kinds of warnings, commercials and corporate narrations are almost always upbeat. You'll need to be full of positive energy when you read them. Not only will it make you seem enthusiastic at an audition, it will help you compete with others who want the same job.

When you're a confident, practiced reader you'll need to consider speed. Radio and television commercials are usually broadcast in ten-, fifteen-, thirty-, or sixty-second formats, with little flexibility. That means if you're cast to read a thirty-second radio spot, you may have to read the spot in exactly thirty seconds. Therefore, you'll want to practice reading ads with a stopwatch. See how long they take to read at your normal rate, then try to stretch or shorten them.

Pay attention to your body language when you read out loud in front of a mirror. You want to *look* as happy as you *sound*, and you need to know how to gesture for emphasis.

Sounds elemental, but on-camera body language is usually a far cry from real life. Because people in commercials are usually shot in medium-wide shots, medium close-ups, and extreme close-ups, you're going to have to learn how to *think and act small*.

The concept of "a little goes a long way" certainly applies to television and film acting. A broad, real-life gesture or expression often looks ridiculous on camera. You must practice giving just a *hint* of an expression in close-up. Just a *slight* gesture will do in almost every situation except extremely wide shots in which your entire body is revealed.

If you contemplate making *print work* a part of your professional repertoire, you'll have to practice holding poses while you wear a wide variety of *believable* expressions. Those expressions are tricky, because the camera doesn't lie. If you are supposed to smile, you must smile with honesty to give the photograph credibility.

When you practice expressions you should call up honest emotion, just as the speaking, moving actor does. The difference is you'll do it without words. The best way to develop this talent is to work in front of a mirror. You'll need plenty of imagination and all your powers of concentration. You must be able to do this effortlessly and unself-consciously if you hope to earn the respect of photographers and ad people.

So practice, practice, practice those expressions. Get comfortable looking—and feeling—happy (with and without showing teeth), sad, pensive, inquisitive, angry, affectionate, and funny. Yes, funny. Those funny expressions you use with friends and relatives might just be ideal for a humorous ad. Realistic expressions don't come easily, so you must practice conscientiously. Be disciplined and take your time.

If calling up honest feelings to generate believable expressions doesn't work for you, read through some of the acting texts listed in Appendix B for pointers to help you get in touch with your feelings. Being in touch with your feelings makes it easier to call them up and use them.

The need for serious preparation thus stated, it's time to say a few words about the actors' unions before we move on to the nuts and bolts of how to start your regional acting career.

On Joining the Actors' Unions

If you launch a regional acting career following the strategy outlined in this book, you will eventually feel ready to expand your base to new market areas within your region, probably including a major market city—Miami, Seattle, Cleveland, Denver, etc.—where union membership may become a necessity. If you succeed on the local and regional levels, joining the Actors' Equity Association, the Screen Actors Guild, or the American Federation of Radio and Television Artists could be a natural next step. You might even want to join all three.

At this writing, the Screen Actors Guild represents approximately seventy-four thousand professional actors and performing artists who work in theatrical and television motion pictures, prime-time television programs, commercials, corporate/industrial films, student and experimental films, and music videos.

The American Federation of Radio and Television Artists represents approximately seventy-eight thousand members nationwide: performers on radio and television broadcasts (including news personnel), videotaped TV programs, corporate/industrial videotapes, and videotaped commercials.

Actors' Equity Association represents approximately thirty-seven thousand professional performers and stage managers nationally who work in Broadway and off-Broadway productions, national tours, resident and nonresident dramatic stock, indoor and outdoor musical stock, dinner theatres, resident theatres, industrial shows, theatre for young audiences, regional professional theatres, cabaret theatre, and some university theatres. And guest-artist arrangements allow Equity performers to appear in certain nonprofessional productions as well.

Whether you should join a union or not is entirely up to you and depends on where you live. It's a difficult decision if you've been successful as a nonunion performer, because joining means you'll have to play the acting game under union rules. Those rules are restrictive if you want to continue acting professionally in your region's smaller towns. For one thing, you'll probably have to charge more for your work. Union minimums can be a high price tag in small towns. And while you'll make more dollars per job under a union contract, there's something to be said for the benefits of nonunion volume.

I made the decision to join AFTRA and SAG when that fearsome word *overexposure* became a reality for me in my home town of Portland, Maine, and I've never regretted it. But the decision to join might not be right for you in *your* region.

If you're successful in your local acting career, you'll eventually be considered "overexposed in the market." These dreaded words mean *trouble*. All of a sudden, the phone stops ringing and your steady commercial, corporate, and print clients begin saying the time has come to make a talent change.

You'll have to do something about it if you want to continue working. That something will be to branch out to larger markets where you'll be a fresh, experienced face and where there will be a greater volume of work available.

Sounds good, huh? Well, in the larger markets things start to get a little tricky for career-minded actors. There's more and better competition for the work, and the casting process is somewhat more complicated. In order to succeed you're going to have to learn a whole new way of doing things, and that new way is slightly different in every market.

In cities like Boston, joining a union or two will be an essential move. However, in Dallas, which is a highly active commercial market, there's cause for pause. Texas is a right-to-work state (or, as union members call it, a right-to-work-for-less state). This means actors don't have to join a union to be eligible to work on union jobs. In right-to-work states union signatories—employers who've signed an agreement with AFTRA or SAG to abide by union rules—can hire non-union members, under certain guidelines. (These guidelines differ slightly for each right-to-work state.) So should you join a union if you live in a right-to-work state? Perhaps, perhaps not.

The important thing to remember here is that the decision is not cut-and-dried. There are many factors at play, and you should take it very seriously. Ask around. Talk to members of the acting community in the market you select. Consult agents and casting agencies. With this professional advice you'll be able to make a decision that's right for you.

Since the great majority of major markets in this country *are* union driven, odds are that sooner or later, probably sooner if you meet with initial success, you'll want to join at least one union. And if you live in a region where there are union offices, you'll be able to get union jobs without actually moving away from home if you're willing to travel.

For specific information on the major actors' unions, including rules, restrictions, how to join, and where to find the regional offices, please see Appendix A.

Reality

While there's no question that almost anyone can qualify for an occasional acting job, be it an extra role or two or a local-color print ad, career-minded actors must understand that it's going to be very difficult to support themselves fully in this profession without working in a combination of fields: television, radio, theatre, corporate television, print, and film. And it's going to take a Herculean work ethic and a positive mental attitude to deal with the inherent competition and rejection that goes with the territory.

Let's look at some statistics. In its most recent survey of member earnings, the Screen Actors Guild reports that of its members who work as principal performers, stunt performers, singers, dancers, extras, voice-over performers, pilots, puppeteers, and models, almost 80 percent earned less than $5,000 under SAG jurisdiction in the survey year. Less than 5 percent of the membership earned more than $50,000 in the same period. AFTRA reports similar statistics for its membership. Actors' Equity Association, in its most recent survey year, reports that only 40 percent of its members worked under AEA contract and that their average earnings were only $10,322.

These statistics reveal that it's extremely difficult to make it as a career actor without another iron or two in the fire. Unless you're independently wealthy, you're going to need a "real" job or two to keep a roof over your head and food on the table while you spend lots of your spare time and most of your energy hustling acting work and getting the training you need.

What support-type jobs do actors seek? Flexible ones. Would you believe waitpersons? How about cab drivers? Commission salespersons? Night work? Some friends of mine—the lucky ones!—have been supported by their spouses. There will, of course, be times when your job will conflict with your acting career, but that's the nature of the beast. So gird your loins and read on.

Chapter

TWO

Getting Ready for Commercials

If you're viewing acting as a possible steady source of income, commercials offer an excellent place to get your feet wet because they are very likely produced near you regularly. Once you get started, you may be able to find steady commercial work.

Local and regional producers today are making commercials using local talent to give their commercials a believable "look." The concept of regional authenticity is growing in the commercial field, and that means those people who look and sound like they're from a particular region are prime candidates for work.

Therefore, whether you're an experienced actor or a raw beginner, there may well be a place for you in local and regional commercials. All you have to do is let the producers of commercials know who you are and what you have to offer. And you don't have to be a union member to find jobs. The truth is, in almost all sections of the country outside our largest cities there's more *nonunion* than union acting work available.

But understand this: if you want to succeed as a commercial actor anywhere, big city or small town, you *must* approach the challenge in a professional manner. You must understand how to project a professional image—an image that says you know who you are and what you're doing.

Professional acting is competitive, even outside New York and Hollywood, and you'll need an edge to succeed.

That edge is difficult to describe, because your uniqueness is what gives it to you. Look at it this way. If you're trying out for the role of a commercial spokesperson against nine others who want it too, and you're all about the same age with equal experience and salable looks, how are *you* going to buck the odds and win?

All things being equal you'll win maybe 10 percent of the time. But if things aren't equal, if you have something extra going for you, something as indefinable as a confident, winning air of professionalism, a look that says, I'm reliable, you can count on me, you might raise that percentage considerably.

Just because you want a career in a less-than-big-time market doesn't mean you shouldn't think and act as professionally there as you would in the big-time ones. Unless you're being considered only for local color, those who are doing the hiring need to know you are the best they can find for the job—on a par with the pros from the big city. It's up to you to convince them that *you are.* How will you do it?

There's an interesting psychology in the regional markets that will prove to be one of your major obstacles. Producers of commercials, even though they need new faces and voices, often think they need better-than-local quality. And they're willing to pay high talent fees to get it, providing they have the budget.

The trend is to produce major projects in the closest *larger* city, using that city's production and talent infrastructure. The producers tend *not* to look in their own backyards. This means, at least at first, that you probably won't be able to compete for the major commercials that are made for your local viewing or listening area. But it's important to understand that when the budget isn't there, when the commercial *must* be made locally with local talent, the ad people still want what they consider "big city" quality. If *you* can provide that, you'll get work. If you're lucky enough to be a type that's in demand, you'll work frequently and make a substantial amount of money.

It's extremely foolhardy to approach this challenge without

realistically preparing yourself to compete as a professional. Why go to all the time and expense if you don't put your best foot forward? Starting an acting career is serious business. Take it seriously and prepare yourself step by step. Start at the beginning, and don't get ahead of yourself.

Discover Your Type

If you decide to aim at commercials, you're going to have to discover your "type." Now, one could argue that there are as many types as there are people. After all, we're all unique, aren't we? Of course we are. But most of us also fall into general categories that ad makers, as well as theatre and movie folks, call *types.*

When commercials—called *spots* in the business—are cast, whether for on-camera roles or voice-overs, "typecasting" rules, because advertisers aim their messages at specific sectors of the viewing or listening audience. Advertisers base their casting decisions on how *they* perceive the majority of people that constitute the market. How do they dress, sound, and move? For example, why cast a group of fashion models for a beer spot or blue-collar types for a wine commercial?

There are many types, and you probably fall into one or more of them. You could be a housewife who's a young mother as pretty and glamorous as a fashion model, with enough authority to project as a businesswoman or even a corporate or product spokeswoman. Or you may be none of these. Do you look like a computer nerd? They are in demand, too.

The only reasonably accurate way to gauge *your* type right now is to seek the honest opinion of others and to watch television to see where you might fit in. Watch the commercials on the air now. Ask yourself, honestly, which roles you could play. If you see yourself again and again in the same category, you may have found your type.

Once you decide that you are indeed a marketable commercial type, it's time to put some personal sales aids together. Let's start with the most important one—*you,* depicted in a commercial photograph.

The Headshot

Everyone will need a high-quality headshot to help get in to meet the people who hire actors, people like producers, directors, casting directors, and agents. Polaroids, family pictures, and shots by friends won't do it. You can get a headshot taken at or close to home at a reasonable cost. The secret is to find the right photographer, a person who specializes in photographing actors, someone who will make sure you get a warm, open, black-and-white headshot that looks like the real you rather than some glamorous ideal.

CHOOSING THE RIGHT PHOTOGRAPHER

Since your headshot will be your most important marketing tool and therefore vitally important to your future success, it is imperative that you make every effort to get the best one possible. To this end I recommend that you choose an experienced professional headshot photographer to take your picture. Do so because these photographers will know how to make you feel comfortable and candid, at least the best ones will, and they understand what actors need in a photograph.

Sadly, I did not follow this advice when I started my regional acting career. I made the mistake of working with a local commercial photographer, who provided me with technically wonderful prints in a totally unacceptable form. Their tone was too dramatic and the lighting too dark. Foolishly I went ahead and had multiple prints made of what I thought to be excellent headshots, only to be informed by several casting people that they just wouldn't work.

Naturally I was concerned. I had wasted valuable time and money on a headshot unsuitable for my goals. What did I do? I made the same mistake a second time. I went to another commercial photographer, showed him the headshot I'd had taken, explained to him what I'd been told was wrong with it, and hired him to take my new picture.

Bad move. Again I was given technically superior prints; but this time the subject matter (me, remember?) was stiff and unnatural. More money and time down the drain.

Finally using my head, I phoned a Boston modeling agent,

one with a reputation for using lots of actors in print advertisements, and asked for the names of professional headshot photographers. I was given three, interviewed them all, and chose the one I felt most comfortable with. You should do the same in your region.

Phone the agents or the SAG office in your region for recommendations. Set aside a couple of days to meet these photographers—be sure to meet them all—to find that special one you feel good about.

During the interviews ask lots of questions. What will be the environment for the picture? How much film will be shot? Who will own the negatives? What will the session cost? How many prints are included in the session fee? Is a makeup artist required? If so, how much will that cost? Are there any guarantees or refunds if you're not satisfied? How long will you have to wait before seeing contact sheets and final prints? Will you have to pay cancellation fees and/or deposits? These questions are always better asked up front to avoid unpleasantness later.

PREPARING FOR THE PHOTO SESSION

Your photo session should be shot only in a studio under controlled lighting conditions. You should expect the photographer to shoot a lot of black-and-white film that will result in a very sharp image. Thirty-five millimeter film is most often used, because you can get more shots for fewer dollars. A good, professional headshot photographer will shoot at least two or three rolls of thirty-six exposures each, which will give you ample possibilities from which to choose. Usually, headshot photographers include one eight-by-ten-inch print in the photo session price. Some will give you two or three.

Be prepared for the photo session. Wear comfortable, nonseasonal, casual clothes. Don't wear black or white. Wear colors of no greater than midrange darkness. Tan, yellow, green, gray, red, brown, and blue translate particularly well into black and white. Texture helps create an impression of warmth of character. For both men and women a mixture of solids with patterns works best. No hats and no plunging necklines. Here are two possible wardrobes for your picture:

MEN

1. Brown or gray tweed sport coat over a blue button-down oxford shirt, open at the neck. Add a tie if you want.
2. Plaid shirt, open at the neck.

WOMEN

1. Red V-necked sweater over light blue, striped button-down.
2. Gray flannel sport coat over pale pink dress blouse.

The focus of the commercial headshot should be on your real looks and personality, not on distractions. Don't wear jewelry; use minimal, natural-looking makeup. Keep in mind that directors and producers tend to prefer traditional looks, so stay away from trendy hairstyles. Headshot photographers, if they know what they're doing, will use even, soft lighting to make sure the shot allows the *real you* to shine through.

Go for as natural a look as you can and keep it energetic, friendly, and full of vitality.

As the photo session progresses, try to relax completely and relate to the camera as though it were a friend with whom you are having a conversation. Talk with the photographer, who's right behind the lens. For at least half the session show your teeth when you smile (without getting too toothy!).

CHOOSING THE RIGHT PHOTOGRAPH

A few days after the photo session your contact sheets should be ready, and you'll be looking at 72, or better yet, 108 tiny pictures of yourself. Now what will you do? How will you choose? Be careful. You don't want to pick one you like and *everybody else* says looks nothing like you. And you don't want to pick one that *you* don't like, either.

Here's a workable approach: using a magnifying glass, look at all the pictures at one sitting and pick the half-dozen smiling shots you like best. Then ask some people you trust—an agent you've met, the photographer, friends, acting teachers, or other actors—to help you decide. Have them look at all the pictures and pick the six shots they like best. The ones that both you and a majority of your helpers like are probably all going to be workable.

Whatever you do, don't mark the six you like best on the contact sheet. This may bias your helpers. Instead, note your favorite shots by row and number within the row. In fact, for your friends' sake, you can number the vertical and horizontal rows so they, too, can give you a list. (A typical listing would be third row, fourth from left.)

Let's say you've narrowed the field to three. Before you make your final selection, ask the photographer to print the finalists in eight-by-ten glossy format, toned for reproduction by a photo service. Remember, you may have to fork out additional money for some of these prints, but it's well worth it.

Sometimes an eight-by-ten blowup looks a lot different than it did as a tiny contact sheet print. Therefore only from the blowups will you be able to choose just the right headshot. Once you've made up your mind, invest in prints.

Just how many headshot duplicates you'll need depends on how much marketing you plan to do, but I recommend a hundred eight-by-ten matte-finish prints as a good starting point. To save money, don't have your photographer make a hundred custom prints for you. That would cost hundreds of dollars. Rather, send your chosen headshot to a quality photo service; they'll do the work for just pennies a copy. Ask your headshot photographer to recommend a couple you can investigate.

For a quality, professional look order your pictures in matte finish with no borders. Have your name printed in an understated type in the lower right- or left-hand corner. (*See the photographs of the successful regional actors in Illustration 1 for an idea of variations of format and style.*)

If you follow this advice and go for conservative, quality, professional photographs, your headshot should serve you well until you change your look (hairstyle, color of hair, nat-

Illustration 1

These pages show some sample commercial headshots.

Patrice Whiting

Joanna Rhinehart

Mark H. Rogers

Photo by Jeff Williams

Anne Washburn

Joe Foster

Photo by Lynn McCann

Photo by Nina Carter

Tom Power

ural aging, etc.). At that point, though, you'll have to get a new one. This cannot be stressed enough: whenever your look changes a new headshot is needed!

You'll also want a new headshot if the one you're using isn't working. Sometimes the one you've chosen just doesn't generate much interest, and you'll have to start the process all over again. This kind of repeat investment of time and money may seem exorbitant, but if you're serious about being a successful commercial actor it's an expenditure you'll have to make. It's almost impossible to land jobs without a good headshot, a headshot that looks like the real you.

Postcards

Once you've nailed down that perfect headshot and invested in eight-by-ten prints, order some postcards from the same photo service that printed your headshots. They serve as an excellent reminder when they arrive in someone's mail. This postcard will need your name and phone number printed on the front below your photograph. Your handwritten or typed messages go on the back.

You can use the same photo you chose for your headshot here, but to broaden your appeal why not select your second choice for this purpose? When people who already have your headshot on hand receive your postcard, they'll get a fresh look at you, a look that might get you jobs.

The Commercial Résumé

Before you hand out your pictures to potential employers, you'll need a résumé that tells them what they need to know about you.

A nifty combination of the headshot and the résumé is the *headsheet,* your eight-by-ten photograph with an eight-by-ten résumé either attached to or printed on the back. This format is easy to handle, and the photo and résumé won't ever get separated from each other.

Your résumé, therefore, must comfortably fit the space, and be packed with as much salable data as possible. For everyone that means essential information such as name, phone numbers (work and home or service), social security number, union affiliations (if any), height, weight, eye and hair colors, and clothing sizes. After that, it's all about what *you* have to offer.

You can land a commercial because of your special skills *alone*. Maybe you're not an actor, but in this case it won't matter. You might qualify for work because of what you can *do*, and may never have to say a line. There are many people who get commercials solely on their "look" (or type). Perhaps you have a certain businessman, farmer, housewife, child, father, or mother look that's salable by itself. Your headsheet should reflect that.

Just think of all the skills you've seen being engaged in on commercial television: playing baseball, basketball, football, tennis, racquetball, handball, squash, golf, table tennis, and billiards; skateboarding, bicycling, and motorcycling; sailing, surfing, waterskiing, swimming, high diving, and scuba diving; performing on parallel bars; juggling, clowning, tightrope walking, and swinging from a trapeze; fly casting and mountain climbing; rodeo and horseback riding; frisbee tossing; baton twirling; roller and ice skating; skeet and trapshooting; sportscar racing; sky diving; painting, sculpting, dancing, fencing, and playing musical instruments; waiting tables, typing, giving manicures, flying airplanes, and narrating fashion shows; the list goes on.

How about physical attributes? Do you look great in a bathing suit? Do you have good legs? Good hair? Good hands? A great or unique voice? Can you do character voices? Accents?

And finally, do you have a passport? It may not be a special skill, but a list of skills is a good place to include this information, which subtly says you're open to travel.

Look at the above lists and ask yourself: Where do I fit? Do I have any related skills or attributes? The chances are you do. But before putting them on your résumé, be honest with yourself. You must never claim a skill or attribute that isn't accurate. Your skill or attribute must be *real*, not marginal. When commercial producers look at your headsheet they need to know they can rely on what's there.

If you think about the vast number of special skills, you'll understand why just about anyone can be right for a commercial at least once in a while.

If you are approaching this from a more career-oriented point of view, your résumé might also include general education, acting-related education and training, amateur and professional theatrical roles played, amateur and professional television and film acting experience, amateur and professional radio experience, and public speaking. See the sample résumés displayed on pages 24–27 for layouts and content suggestions that might work for you. You'll notice that they all break the information down into categories, with the most important information listed first in each category.

An important point to remember is that your résumé should never appear sloppy or hastily put together. It should be attractive and appealing, not to mention easy to read. It's purpose is to sell *you*. In many cases people you have not met or will not meet will read it, and it *must* project you in a favorable light. Have your résumé professionally printed. The cost is minimal. And design it so that your strengths are emphasized.

Is there information you should *not* include on your résumé? Most definitely, yes. For your own protection, consider whether or not you want to put your home address on the résumé; you never know where that résumé is going to go. And do not list your commercial credits (once you have them) or anything politically controversial on your résumé.

If you want to include a commercials category, do it this way: COMMERCIALS: Conflicts on request. This tells your prospective employers you have experience doing commercials but doesn't present them with the immediate conflict that occurs when you have a commercial currently running in direct competition with the spot for which you're being considered.

To illustrate, let's say that two years ago you appeared in a television spot for a local car dealer that ran for just thirteen weeks. Now your headsheet is sitting on the desk of some ad exec who's casting a spot for another car dealer. Although you no longer have a conflict, if the exec sees your previous car commercial listed on your résumé you probably won't be considered for this one because you'll be *perceived* as having a conflict.

The "COMMERCIALS: Conflicts on request" designation will keep you in the running, and when you're asked whether you have a conflict you can say no.

The warning about politically related work stems from a mistake I made early in my career. I was hired by a local production company to host a video presentation highlighting the virtues of Maine's only nuclear power plant. After completing the project I immediately listed *Maine Yankee* under the INDUSTRIAL FILMS heading on my résumé. About a year later, during an audition for a newspaper commercial, the director asked me whether the film had been pro nuclear power. When I answered yes, he informed me the audition was over. I lost that job for reasons that had nothing to do with acting ability.

So leave controversy out of your résumé. Stress the positive and pay attention to the benefits of a good design. And don't forget to update your résumé every time you can add something that will reflect positively on your professional image. (*Some résumé examples are shown in Illustration 2.*)

You might say at this point: Hey! I'm not going to Hollywood here, I just want to do local and regional commercials. Why do I have to do all this stuff? Because it is the professional thing to do. Since there is always plenty of competition for local and regional commercials, why not approach the whole business in the most professional way you can?

Other Things You'll Need

Acting, like any other job, requires the tools of the trade. To begin, you'll need a basic wardrobe, dependable transportation, and an answering machine; when you seriously start going after commercials, add demo tapes, stationery, and a professional-looking holder in which to lug your headsheets around.

WARDROBE

Your wardrobe is important. You'll need an outfit to wear that plays well to your personal type for interviews, auditions, and, of course, on the job. But how far should you go at first?

Illustration 2

NANCY GAHAGAN

Phone 617-555-6665

Height: 5'8"
Weight: 130
Hair: Blonde
Eyes: Blue
Voice: Soprano

THEATRE

Taken in Marriage	Annie	Butler University Theatre
Ghosts	Mrs. Alving	
Phaedra	Phaedra	
Seascape	Sarah	
My Sister in this House	Christine	
Quilters	Janie	North Shore Music Theatre
Godspell	Peggy	Charity Productions
Gondoliers	Guilia	North Shore Light Opera Co.
Pirates of Penzance	Kate	
Waiting for Willy	Sallie Mae	Priscilla Beach Theatre
Marshall Jones		

TRAINING

Acting: Butler University Theatre, BA Theatre
           North Shore Music Theatre
               Judy Braha · Acting
               Pat Dougan · Acting in Commercials
           Barton Square Theatre
           Jeannie Lindheim

Voice: Patricia Tamigini
           Laurel Goetzinger
           Robert Ingari

Dance: Marblehead School of Ballet (Jazz, Ballet, Modern)
           North Shore Civic Ballet Co. (two year company member)
           Butler University (Ballet, Jazz, Theatre Dance)
           Joffrey School of Ballet (Ballet)

DIALECTS

Standard British, Irish, French, Southern, Midwestern, New York

SPECIAL SKILLS

Speak French, Children's Theatre, Creative Dramatics, Lighting Design, Flautist, Singing, Dancing

This is a clear, well-formatted beginning actor's résumé. Since the actor has no film, TV, corporate/industrial, or commercial credits, her résumé reflects theatre, training, and special skills.

John Michael Raftery

Height: 5' 11"   Hair Color: Black
Weight: 155   Skin Tone: Fair
Eye Color: Green

——————— A C T I N G   E X P E R I E N C E ———————

FILM & TELEVISION

Principal Character: WCVB-TV "Friends" promo for Natalie Jacabson
Principal Character: Public Service Announcement for the Governor's Highway Patrol
　　　　　　　　　　against drunk driving
Principal Character: Industrial Video for the Liberty Tree Mall
Principal Character: Industrial Video for the Diet Workshop "Twi-Lite Zone" promotion
Principal Character: National commercial for the Diet Workshop
Principle Character: Industrial Video against under age drinking for the Restaurant
　　　　　　　　　　Association of America
　　　　　Extra: "The Kennedys and Fitzgeralds" mini-series

THEATER

Spring 1990   *Witness for the Prosecution*   Mayhew   Needham Community Theater

PRINT WORK

National magazine advertisement for John Hancock Life Insurance
Newspaper ad for Jordan Marsh
Newspaper and catalog work for Grover Cronin Inc.

——————— E D U C A T I O N ———————

Acting I & II with Susan McGinley at U. Mass Boston
Advanced Scene Study with Linda Bissesti at U. Mass. Boston
Intermediate Acting with Bill Kelley at the New Ehrlich Theater
Workshop for Television Acting at the Cameo Agency

This beginning actor's résumé is well designed too. Note the bold box around the information and the horizontal lines used to separate categories.

(Illustration 2 continued)

SALLY MONROE

Vital Statistics
Blue Eyes • Brown Hair
110 lbs. • 5'5" tall

Present Address

Stage

Susy	Wait Until Dark	Mary Moody Northen, Austin, TX
Mary	How the Other Half Loves	Mary Moody Northen, Austin, TX
Suzanna	Bedroom Farce	Central Mall Dinner Theatre, Lawton, OK
Nora	A Doll's House	The Little Theatre, Lawton, OK
Terry	Extremities	The Little Theatre, Lawton, OK
Annie	The Miracle Worker	The Little Theatre, Lawton, OK
Barnaby	The Matchmaker	Cameron University Theatre, Lawton, OK
Heroine	Shameful Shooting	Oklahoma State University, Stillwater, OK
Stepmother	Hansel and Gretel	Playhouse in the Park, Lawton, OK
Gertie	Oklahoma	Canterbury Theatre, Michigan City, IN
Agnes	All American	Canterbury Theatre, Michigan City, IN
Celia	As You Like It	Cameron University Theatre, Lawton, OK
Gladys	Carnival	Canterbury Theatre, Michigan City, IN
Violet	Second Street Hotel	Newbury Street Theatre, Boston, MA

Television

- Spokesperson for training films for *McDonald's*, Oklahoma City, OK and Lawton, OK
- Talent in local *Total Maintenance* commercial by KFDX Channel 3, Wichita Falls, TX
- Talent in PSA's for Cameron University Theatre

Education

Cameron University, Lawton, OK 1989
Bachelor of Fine Arts Degree
Major: Theatre: Acting/Directing
Major: Communications: Public Relations/Organizational

Awards and Affiliations

- Aamco Acting Award, Regional American College Theatre Fest
- Irene Ryan Acting Award, Oklahoma Region
- Outstanding Actress, Cameron University
- President, Chapter Alpha Psi Omega Theatre Fraternity
- Artist in Residence, Lawton Public Schools

Special Skills

Ventriloquism, Clowning, Mime, Roller skating, Dialects.

Excellent experience as Marketing Coordinator of *McDonald's Corp.* and Group Sales Director of Boston's *Shear Madness.*

References

Dr. David Fennema Cameron University Theatre, Lawton OK (405) 581-2346
David Graham Canterbury Theatre, Chicago, IL (messages) (312) 338-7615
Melba Mischler Mary Moody Northen Equity Theatre, Austin, TX (512) 448-8484

This eye-catching résumé is another designed to make a relative beginner look like a seasoned professional. Again, the emphasis is on theatre, but education, special skills, and even references are included. As this actor's professional credits multiply, the references, awards and affiliations, and some of the college theatre credits can be omitted.

EDWARD MASON
SAG/AFTRA/AEA

Service: Height: 5'9"   Hair: Blonde
                      Weight: 165   Eyes: Blue

TELEVISION

SPENSER	Dale (Featured)	David Whorf, Dir.
DEADLY FORCE	#2 Cop	Michael Miller, Dir.
SPENSER	Gus "	Richard Colla, Dir.
T.J. HOOKER	Frank "	Rick Kolbe, Dir.
UNDER THIS SKY	Cowboy "	Randa Haines, Dir.
THE VISITOR	Johnson "	Buz Alexander, Dir.
MILLER'S COURT	Ed Robbins (Lead)	Bill Lowell, Dir.
A LITTLE DEATH	Ferondo (Lead)	Alan Ritsko, Dir.

FILM

THE VERDICT	Widow's Son (Featured)	Sidney Lumet, Dir.
THE DOZENS	Sonny (Lead)	Randall Conrad/ Christine Dall, Dirs.
FLASHBACK	John (Featured)	Georgia Morris, Dir.
PAWN	Harlen Cook (Featured)	Bill Walker, Dir.

THEATRE

PICNIC	Hal	Monomey Theatre
GEO. OF A HORSE DREAMER	Jason	Boston Arts Group
THE OTHER CINDERELLA	Danny	Charles Playhouse, Boston
COMEDY OF ERRORS	Aegeon	Loeb Theatre, Cambridge
OH DAD, POOR DAD	Head Bell Boy	Boston Arts Theatre

COMMERCIALS & PRINT

List upon request

TRAINING

ACTING--Peter Frish/Jose Quintero/John Bottoms/Jack Phillips
VOICE--Bill Lacey
MOVEMENT--Adrenne Hawkins/Dorothy Anderson

DIALECTS/ACCENTS

Irish, British, Southern, Boston, New England, Swedish

SPECIAL SKILLS

Impersonations: Lancaster, Brando, Newman etc., Poetry Recitals/Readings, Boxing, Football, Swimming, Snow Skiing, Fencing, Tennis, Squash, some Gymnastics, Walking on Hands, Standing on Hands, U.S. Passport.

DANCE

Jazz and Modern

VIDEO TAPE AVAILABLE UPON REQUEST

Here's a regional résumé to which we can all aspire. It reveals strong credits in television, film, theatre, and training; it highlights what this actor can do with proficiency; and it is clearly and simply designed.

Common sense says that the wardrobe you use to get work should double as street clothing. Your type is your type, right? If you dress well for it, those who count will think your clothes are fine. Two or three outfits should be plenty until they've all been used on jobs.

Before you buy anything, look in your closet to see what you have now that will work for you. Both men and women will need a suit as well as casual clothes in light to midtone colors. No blacks, no whites. Pastel shirts under tweed sport coats are great. Tan slacks with conservative plaid jackets look comfortable. In summer have some polo shirts around, but not the kind with the cute little emblems. Remember, you're not selling clothes.

Once you've put your wardrobe together, always have it ready to go. Keep it separate from your everyday wear. Most actors reserve a closet for their working clothes so they're easy to get at and safe from other family members who might "borrow" them—a constant problem in my home.

MAKEUP

A *makeup kit* adds to your professional image. In fact, when you're interviewing for a job you may be asked whether you can do your own makeup. A yes means that the director/producer can save some money and will give you yet another edge when you compete for work on low-budget productions. But remember this: if you answer yes, you must be proficient at applying your makeup. This means you—particularly you men out there—are going to have to practice making yourself up.

For television purposes, a little makeup goes a long way. Both men and women, unless they are doing character makeup, such as a witch or clown, can get by very well with good-quality over-the-counter basics such as a foundation that matches your complexion, blush if you need it, eyeliner (be wary of black eyeliner, it reads very hard on-camera) and translucent powder, pressed or loose. Women will also need lipstick and mascara.

This basic kit, used effectively, should do it until you work with a makeup artist.

If you need advice on how to apply makeup for television,

consult a local college or university instructor who teaches makeup. He or she will know what you should do and will no doubt recommend specific products for you to use.

TRANSPORTATION

Getting to and from the many appointments you'll set up demands *reliable transportation*. The nature of the regional actor's markets means you won't be able to rely completely on public transportation, so a decent car will help you manage your time efficiently. You'll be able to get to outlying areas as quickly as your local speed limits allow. Reliability often makes the difference in getting that first break.

The ad business operates at a frenetic pace. Casting (and other) decisions are often made at the last minute. It's not unusual for actors to get a call late in the afternoon for a job early the next morning at a production studio five miles north of the center of town.

Believe this: *there are no acceptable excuses for missing a work call.* None. If you're reputed to be unreliable, you're finished. That's it.

ANSWERING MACHINE

An *answering machine* with beeperless remote will help you keep on top of things without missing any opportunities. Although you won't get too many calls at first, *check in regularly and answer any calls promptly*. It's never too soon to establish that habit. Actors who live in major cities often opt for answering services, but that's expensive and it isn't really necessary on the local and regional levels.

After a while you'll find that work calls come in at odd times, sometimes just an hour or two before your services are required. Therefore, if you have a regular job, put your work number on the machine.

The idea here is to be easy to reach. By answering all calls quickly and letting people know where you are, you'll establish a good availability profile. You want producers to be saying, Let's get Bill Steele for this last-minute job. He's easy to track down.

The message you record on your answering machine can

be as creative as you want to make it, but the best approach is the straight one. Here's a message that won't turn anyone off: Hi, this is Bill Steele. Please leave your message when you hear the beep and I'll get back to you as soon as I can. Thanks. A message like this works best because it's short (only about ten seconds), and it isn't cute. Those who phone you repeatedly will appreciate this no-nonsense approach.

The answering machine is no place to demonstrate your acting ability.

DEMO TAPES

If you want to do radio and TV commercials based on more than your look or skills alone, you'll need an audio *demo tape* that shows your vocal range. On your tape you should read several short pieces of ad copy demonstrating varying energy levels; at least one or two should be set to music. Your tape should also include at least one straight narration piece, so corporate and audiovisual producers can also consider you.

If you've never been in commercials and therefore have no professionally produced work, don't despair. Look in the yellow pages under audio production services and call all the studios until you find one that has helped others make demo tapes. Tell them you're just starting out, and let them take it from there. They'll know exactly what to do, and they can often offer highly constructive criticism. Bring with you some ad copy you like from magazines just in case the audio production service you choose doesn't provide material for you to read.

Keep your demo tape short—no longer than three minutes. A cassette format is best. Cassettes are much cheaper than reel to reel, and their quality gets better all the time.

Voice-over actors use demo tapes the way on-camera actors use headsheets. You'll need cassettes in bulk, and you can buy them that way. The recording-studio people can probably steer you to reliable sources of supply. Start with a hundred, and buy a cheap tape deck with two sets of heads so you can make your own duplicates. A deck should cost less than the studio's fee to make the dupes for you.

Do you sing? There's lots of money to be made in commercial jingles. It pays to have a separate tape that sells your singing talents. Don't bother with classical pieces—commercials are upbeat. Go for contemporary music that requires a good vocal range and get-up-and-go.

Once you've been cast in some on-camera roles, put together a video demo on half-inch VHS tape. Again, keep it short—around three minutes in length. And make sure it has plenty of variety.

STATIONERY

You'll need *stationery* when sending headsheets and demo tapes through the mail. Have yours professionally printed on quality paper, but don't go overboard. Keep it simple: just your name, address, and phone number until you have a track record.

PORTFOLIO

When you meet ad people for the first time you'll want to hand them your demo tape and headsheet, so get something attractive and businesslike in which to carry them. A small *portfolio* that can also hold and protect other photographs is fine. This item will prove particularly necessary if you seek print work, which is discussed in Chapter 7.

APPOINTMENT BOOK

Obviously, you must have an appointment book to keep track of who you're going to see and where you've been. This is absolutely essential. Buy one that has plenty of room to make notations. Make a habit of listing your daily expenses, including your mileage. This information will come in handy at tax time.

Now for the real business of acting—looking for work.

Chapter
THREE
Looking for Work in Commercials

Commercials are made by advertising agencies, radio and television stations, and production houses. They are also, though less frequently, produced by the advertisers themselves. Your goal is to land any commercial work that's available.

Your search for that work will lead you to the realization that, yes, more time is spent looking for commercial work than working in commercials.

Once you make up your mind to try acting in commercials, set a reasonable time frame in which to start finding jobs. Many New York and Los Angeles actors spend several years before they taste success, but it shouldn't take that long if you stay close to home. Nevertheless, unless you're among the lucky few, lightning won't strike immediately. It's going to take some time before you see results. So relax and enjoy it; call it paying your dues. The secret is to practice the three P's. Be *persistent.* Be *patient.* And keep your attitude *positive.*

Sounds *easy,* doesn't it? Well it won't after several rejections. Don't let it get you down, your turn will come.

Some worry is normal. Rejection *is* negative, and actors hate it. It's impossible not to get discouraged. But it's imperative not to give in to those negative feelings or you'll defeat yourself. And never let those feelings show as you beat the bushes for work. If you do, the decision makers won't want anything to do with you. Remember, everybody loves a winner, so look and act like one whether you're winning or not.

The most important tip in this book may just be, as a popular deodorant commercial put it, *"Never let 'em see you sweat."* If you look nervous and desperate for work, you probably won't get it. The job will go to an actor who at least *appears* relaxed. Of course, it *will* help if you have a financial cushion or a flexible or part-time job to make money less of a problem. In any case, your attitude should always be, I'll give it my best shot; after all, what have I got to lose.

That said, let's see how a beginner can find work.

Advertising Agencies

When it comes to sheer volume, *advertising agencies* produce the most commercials by far, so they should be at the top of your hit list. They tend to pay better than other producers because they work for a percentage of creative (including talent) costs. Your goal should be to meet and sell yourself to the commercial producers in every agency in your area. The commercial producers make casting *recommendations*, but most casting *decisions* are made by committee, and over this you will have no control. But it still won't hurt to have a producer put in a good word for you.

How do you find out who these producers are and where they work? You could look up the names and numbers of all the agencies in your area, phone them, and ask to speak with their producers. But there's a better way.

Start by watching television and listening to the radio for a few days. Pay particular attention to the morning local news, the 6:00 P.M. local news, the 11:00 P.M. local news, and any local sporting events that are broadcast. Be alert for the locally produced spots. What are they likely to be? Local banks, newspapers, food stores, department stores, clothing stores, car dealerships, dairies, tire warehouses, lumber yards, glass replacement centers, schools and colleges, insurance agencies, law firms, state lotteries, drug stores, appliance warehouses, and so on. List the companies in your area that fall into these categories. Then, using the yellow pages, call these businesses directly and ask to speak with the director of advertising. This person works closely with the agency and knows the names of everyone you need to contact.

Then, if you're marketing just your look or special skills, send your headsheet to the names you've been given. When the search goes out for what you have to offer, they'll come to you.

When you want to pursue commercial acting on a wider scale, you'll need to go to them. But don't try to meet the ad directors, because the advertising agency producers are likely to resent it. They may decide you've gone beyond your bounds and are too pushy. (You're *supposed* to be pushy if you want work, but you have to keep your pushiness low-keyed!)

The only time it's appropriate to meet the director of advertising of a company or a business is when they produce their own advertising campaigns and don't use the services of an agency. If you have the director of advertising on the phone, and he or she has just told you they don't use an agency, request an appointment. Say you are a new actor in town, that you have a photograph, résumé, and voice demo, and add that you'd appreciate a short meeting so that you can be kept in mind for future radio and television spots.

If your voice is confident and pleasant, your telephone personality may "sell" the listener on your ability. He or she may agree to see you, or at least encourage you to send in your headsheet and voice demo.

While you have advertising directors on the phone, ask them not only the names of the agencies they use but also the names of the contacts, known as account executives, through whom they work at those agencies. Account executives are overall managers of all the advertising for that particular client. Also request the names of the agency's in-house TV and radio producers and directors. Smaller, local agencies may not employ in-house producers and directors; a senior art director may bear this responsibility. Having these names will save you time and help you reach those in a position to help you.

When you phone the ad agencies, ask for the people whose names you've received. Your call will be directed to them or to their secretaries.

If you reach a secretary, request your target by name. You will probably be asked who you are and whom you represent; state your name and say that you represent yourself. If pressed further, add that you are a new actor in town and would like an appointment. Be very businesslike but tactful.

The secretary may put you right through, but more likely you'll hear something like, I'm sorry, he's in a meeting; or, I'm afraid she's just stepped away from her desk. May I take a message? Your answer? Yes, please tell her that Bill Steele called. What time would be convenient for me to call back? You'll be given a time. Be sure to call back at that time. Maybe you'll get through, maybe you won't; but keep trying until it's obvious that the person won't talk to you. Stay as pleasant and professional as you can during these forays. Never alienate a secretary! Many secretaries today will be producers tomorrow.

If you know you won't get an appointment, ask whether you may mail in your headsheet and/or a demo tape.

If and when you *do* reach your target by phone (and you probably will when you deal with the smaller agencies) use the same sales pitch you use with everyone else. Just say you're a new actor in town and that you want to establish yourself with the local agencies. Add that you have photos and demonstration materials. Then request a brief appointment.

The voice on the other end may say fine, or you may hear, We don't meet with actors, just put your stuff in the mail. Follow this lead. At least you've chatted in person; you're off to a start.

If an appointment *is* granted, be sure to get there on time. Don't overdress, but do, at least, wear a sport coat and tie or a blazer and a business blouse. (The tendency is to wear your dress-up clothes, and the secret is *simplicity*.) Smile, and try to look and feel relaxed. If you have no professional acting credits, don't tell advertising people that you're trying to break in until you're asked the inevitable, So, tell me about your experience. At that point stress the experience you've had meeting the public—sales, working behind a counter, public speaking.

Be honest about your situation, and point out your educational preparation. You'll have to sell your potential, which should be obvious from your personality, your appearance, your professionalism, and your demo tape. At the end of the "interview" (that's what it really is) remind your target that you are always ready to come in for an audition. If they like you personally and/or are impressed with the way you look and sound, you'll be asked back. After the interview, go home and write a thank-you letter on your business stationery. You need to say that you enjoyed the meeting and that you hope to hear from them soon.

When you are asked to submit your materials by mail include a letter something like this:

Dear Producer or Account Executive:
  Here are a headshot, my résumé, and a current audio demo tape. Thank you in advance for looking these materials over. I will call you after a couple of weeks to make sure my materials arrived safely and to request an appointment.
Sincerely yours,

A letter like this—short and to the point—has a good chance of being read. The reader will probably shrug and say what the heck, and then look at your picture. Assuming the picture's okay, your tape might be played. If your voice has the "right" sound as far as the listener is concerned, you will surely be considered for work and will undoubtedly get an appointment.

Here's a very important warning: do not call within days of sending your materials. Wait at least two weeks! That way you'll be less annoying and will not appear anxious.

If when you call two weeks later you find your materials have not been evaluated, nonchalantly say something like: Fine. I was just checking. I'll call you back in a couple of weeks. Try just two more times, waiting a minimum of two weeks between each try. If that doesn't work, communicate by mail in the future until *you* are contacted. By sending

your headsheet regularly, once every six months or so, you
may land an interview—or better yet—a job.

If you make more than three tries to get through, you'll
just alienate the people you need most. These folks tend to
have long memories for voices, names, and faces. You can't
afford to be in the doghouse even before you've met them!

As simple as these approaches to contacting local advertisers and their agencies may sound, they will help you get
your foot in the door. The rest rides on your voice, type,
and ability.

Radio and Television Stations

Many actors—even experienced ones—aren't aware that radio and television stations have production departments that
act as agencies for companies and businesses. While they
don't offer complete advertising services, they do offer radio
or television spot services from creation through production.

Many small companies and businesses who want to advertise on radio and television, but who do not want to pay the
extra percentages to regular advertising agencies, choose
these in-house services because they are *much* less expensive. Typically, a station will charge an advertiser only for radio or television *time* and will throw in creative services at no
fee.

RADIO STATIONS

Radio stations will also toss in voice talent, using one of their
in-house on-air personalities, at minimal cost. But when the
client requests a voice that is not associated with the station,
outside talent must be brought in. The production manager
is the one who finds that talent, and that's whom you want
to contact.

When you phone, ask for the production manager's name,
and then ask to speak with him or her. Use the same techniques I've already outlined if you don't get through right
away. Once you make contact, say you're a new voice talent
in the area, that you're nonunion, have a demo tape, and
are willing to work at area minimums in order to break in.
(You union actors should offer to work at scale—minimum

rates set by the union for the type of work performed.) That's right. Tell *these* people you're trying to break in. If you have a marketable voice, the words "break in" and "area minimums" will strike a positive chord.

Many radio stations do not operate under union contract, which means that they pay people what *they* want, not what the union requires for its members. (When they want to use union members they pay them through a paymaster such as Broadcast Residuals and Talent in New York, a company that exists solely to act as a financial funnel for union-franchised jobs.) This is great news for the beginner. So if you're willing to work at area minimums, these radio stations are likely to consider you almost immediately.

What are area minimums? Well, it depends on what you're asked to do and which region you're in. But it shouldn't be too hard to find out.

Ask your instructors of professional acting classes or faculty members at local college or university theatre departments for the names of some established regional actors you can approach for advice. When you contact these people tell them your status. Based on your level of experience, they should be able to suggest a rate of pay that won't frighten your potential employer off and will also protect the integrity of the profession. This will also ensure that you will not alienate the existing acting community you're hoping to penetrate.

As you gain professional experience and are sought more for your voice quality than your price, you can gradually raise your rates, eventually reaching your region's maximums.

But remember this: if you have a good voice and can read commercial copy with personality and authority, you'll be amazed at the number of local radio spots you'll do if you keep your price down. And as the number of spots you do goes up, so will your bank balance. Therefore, it might be wise go slowly in the rate-raising department.

TELEVISION STATIONS

Network affiliate—ABC, NBC, and CBS—stations do *lots* of inexpensive, local commercials that can be a great source of income for you, and independent and cable television stations also have in-house production departments that put together commercials. In direct contrast to radio stations, all of these television stations almost always use outside talent. They don't use their own on-air personalities because of actual or perceived conflicts of interest, so the way is paved for your entry.

Again, start with the production director. Cite your inexperience and willingness to work for area minimums until you develop a track record. Because local TV stations produce commercials for clients who don't want the expense of hiring an agency, inexpensive but capable talent fits right into their requirements.

When you speak with the production director, ask whether you can come to the station and be videotaped reading commercial copy. This is a common practice, and far more television stations than not maintain a library of their own talent tapes. Each time a new talent request is made, the tapes will be viewed in search of likely candidates, so you'd better be on them! (This applies to union actors as well.)

Also, be sure you give the production director several headsheets so he can pass them on to his clients. He'll appreciate that because, although it's self-serving, it *is* professional.

Of the three types of television stations, start with the independents. They usually carry a lot of local programming, show plenty of films, and have the most hours slotted for local advertising.

Local cable stations are also a good starting point because they appeal to advertisers with small budgets. In addition, they are an excellent vehicle for the beginner to get on-air experience other than commercials. They're always looking for locally produced shows—talk shows, for example—that they can sell to local advertisers. And those local shows need inexpensive (would you believe free?) talent. Offer your services to the cable companies in your area in any and all talent categories. You may find yourself hosting a local talk show or acting in a local playwright's new play.

Production Houses

Corporations nationwide now use television for a large percentage of their internal and external communications requirements. (Chapter 5 examines corporate television and its implications for actors in detail.) Because of the explosive growth of both commercial and corporate television over the past three decades, independent production services have flourished. Today, almost every city or town large enough to support an advertising or corporate community will have an independent production house, sometimes several. These production houses are prime sources of television commercial opportunities.

These businesses cater to ad agencies and corporations that want to work on their projects without being subject to the scheduling constraints of television stations. They offer production studios, directors, technical personnel, and equipment—everything to produce a commercial or corporate video, from soup to nuts.

Look in the yellow pages under television production, video production services, or audio production for those near you; go through the same cold-call procedure already outlined in detail. Again, you're after the producers. Tactfully ask the person who answers your initial call for an appropriate name and then request to speak to him or her. Explain your situation and request an appointment. If an appointment is not granted, ask whether it would be appropriate to send in your headsheet and demo tape. They'll say yes.

Just as television stations like to have talent tapes on hand, production houses do too. They are frequently asked to recommend talent and are always watching for good new actors. Being able to suggest new faces and voices makes them look good to their clients, who are usually the advertising agencies you've pitched. Your demo tape will help them do that.

When the advertising producer, who's already either met with or heard about you, hears that the production house recommends you, your chances have improved significantly.

You should definitely charge more for television than radio

commercials, no matter where they are produced; but, again, you'll at first want to keep your fees at the area minimums (which you'll have discovered by talking with other actors). You'll be charging less for a voice-over (that's when you speak but are not seen) than an on-camera performance.

Back in the early seventies I was cast as a farmer in a local TV spot for a meat-processing business. All I had to do was look at the camera while ringing a dinner bell, and say "Come and get 'em!" My fee: fifty dollars and ten pounds of product—in this case, hot dogs. Now that might not sound like much today, but as a struggling teacher/actor trying to raise six kids I didn't even think of turning it down. Admittedly, it wasn't much of a spot and the fee was rock bottom—fifty dollars *was* the area minimum in Portland back then—but that spot helped get me going.

For a nonspeaking, unidentifiable on-camera role—in other words, being an *extra*—take whatever you're offered. Many experienced actors won't do extra work, but it's a way for you to get acquainted with producers and directors who may have principal roles for you later on. *Do not turn down extra work when you are starting out.*

Keeping your rates at established area minimums will get you work if you have what the job requires. Try to get more money if your spots will air in more than one city. And never tell anyone your rates until you're specifically asked. Try to get them to make an offer first. With a little luck this offer will be higher than the area minimum.

The Casting Interview

When the ad agency, television or radio station, or production house actually has a spot for which you're being considered, you'll be invited to a casting interview.

This interview is usually set up so the producer/director can look at and listen to you in light of the spot in question. Are you the right type? Does your voice work for the ad concept? If not, you won't be cast. But don't miss the opportunity to show the producer/director that you are capable and professional. This helps keep you in the running for future jobs.

Dress for the role and hand over your headsheet and demo tape when you get there. Make sure you say when you're available and indicate your willingness to take what comes along. But don't grovel. Remember, if you act like you need the work, you probably won't get it. If you are asked to read for a speaking part, try to do it with a sense of spontaneity. The producer/director will want even the most stilted copy read conversationally so it sounds real. To prepare for this kind of cold reading, acting classes are, again, highly recommended.

Auditions

Ad agencies often set up auditions at which several actors are asked to compete for each role. Usually you, and any other actors who are competing against you, will read the proposed commercial on videotape so agency staff can review it; they'll make their decision based on what's on the tape.

You'll be asked to appear at the taping site at a specific time. You will then be asked to read the role for which you are being considered. If the part requires just a look or a special skill, you won't have to read anything. In this case you'll probably just be interviewed.

When you arrive you'll no doubt see several other actors, and that can be intimidating at first. Try to ignore any negative feelings, and read the script you're given. Get familiar with it. Read it out loud, even if there are other actors lurking about, so you can get used to the words and handle them smoothly. This will give you all the preparation you'll need for the actual taping.

When it's your turn to audition, you'll be taken into a room where there's a camera and lights and perhaps a few people in addition to the producer/director. If there are other people there, they will be from the agency. Introductions will be made all around. You may also be accompanied by another actor or two if there are multiple characters in the commercial.

You'll be asked to stand in a certain spot and face the camera. If they don't ask you to rehearse the reading before the tape rolls, you may—and probably should—ask for a rehearsal. You're bound to get some feedback and direction that will help when you're on tape. You'll read either from the script in your hand or from cue cards set up beside the camera. Either way, try to make as much eye contact with the camera as you comfortably can without stumbling over your words.

Lights! Camera! Action! Your knees start to shake. The camera person will say, Slate your name. What do you do now? You look directly into the camera lens and tell the viewer your name. Some actors slate with a smile, some with perk, some straight, some humorous. Why don't *you* try, Hi, I'm . . . in a friendly but straight, smiling manner. You can't go wrong by being conservative.

After the slate, read the spot as conversationally as you can. You may get only one chance to read, but in most cases you'll have more than one read-through, or *take*. Each time you go through the copy, try your best to alter your reading according to the directions that are inevitably given. Common audition direction includes: Warm it up a little; Be more conversational; Give it some energy. When you hear comments like this, they're more than suggestions. They're a test to determine whether or not you can "take direction."

Taking direction demands versatility on your part, and is one of the skills you can work on in your acting classes. Commercial directors want to work with actors who know how to alter their style on demand and can make interpretive changes easily. It's important to understand that in the world of commercials, actors are expected to deliver lines the way the director wants in very specific terms. Actors who come to the commercial shoot locked in to one rigid interpretation are asking for trouble.

Once there's enough on tape to determine your flexibility and type, you'll be thanked. Return the thanks and shake hands (if convenient) and leave with a confident smile (even though you feel like a bowl of jelly). You've done all you can. If you're the one for the job you'll probably get it. If not, you won't. Try not to worry about it.

Here's some important advice. Don't sit around waiting for the phone to ring. Get out and look for new opportunities;

go skiing; exercise; do anything you can that will help you forget that you even auditioned. That way, if you don't get cast, your disappointment will be minimized because you haven't been dwelling on the possibility of failure.

Early in my acting career I never took this advice. I used to sit by the phone for hours wondering why it wasn't ringing. What had gone wrong in the audition? Why didn't they like me? My ego was on the line. I did this for a long time, until a successful actor friend of mine took me aside and gave me the lowdown. "You're suffering from the 'disease,' " he said, "and there's only one cure. You've got to have other important interests in your life that will take your mind off the phone."

He told me that I'd know I had successfully conquered this actors' malady when I was able to forget what I had auditioned for within twenty-four hours. Over the years I've trained myself to do just that, at least most of the time. And you can, too.

Sometimes decisions take quite a while. So if you don't hear from the producer/director immediately, it may mean that no decision has been made. Sometimes commercial projects are shelved for a while or canceled altogether. If you sit around wondering what's going on, you may be sitting for a long time. Much better to get busy with something else and forget it.

If a decision isn't made on the basis of the first audition tape (although with local spots it usually is), you might get a callback. Then you will be taped again and have to wait again.

Callbacks

A *callback* is exactly that, a call back. It's an invitation to audition again for the same commercial. It means they liked you the first time around and that you're still under consideration.

The best way to approach the callback is to do everything the same way you did it the first time. This is easier if you take notes before and after each audition. Write down what you wore, right down to the shoes, and try to describe the material and your performance. There may be some time between the initial taping and the callback.

Wear the same clothes unless you're asked to wear something else, and read the copy in the same conversational way. You'll probably be taped again and given more direction.

Many actors—I'm one of them—don't like to audition. But it's important to audition every chance you get, even if you're not the right type for the role—just for practice. As you do it again and again your skills will improve and you'll learn to relax.

Follow-Ups

Checking in is a form of *follow-up*, an essential actor activity. Follow-ups include—in addition to checking in—letters, postcards, new headsheets, and demo tapes.

Checking in should involve no more than a fast phone call in which you call someone *you've seen* and say something like, Hi, this is Bill Steele. I'm just checking to see whether you've got anything for me. It's a short, friendly business call, not a bothersome chat. Don't call anyone more than every few weeks. Don't become a pest.

Letters and postcards are the only way to thank people for interviews and auditions. Send one every time until you are really known, and then you won't have to, because you'll see your employers all the time and will be able to say thanks in person.

Whenever you update a résumé or get a new headshot—remember, that's every time your look changes—it's a great excuse to contact *everyone* you've met to give them one. Do it by mail and include a short letter saying you hope to hear from them soon.

Follow-ups take time, but they keep your name in front of your potential employers.

National Advertisers, Regional Spots

As I noted in Chapter 1, national advertisers now produce an increasing number of regional ads to take advantage of lower costs and authentic locations. Don't be surprised if a national advertiser decides to make a regional spot in your area. When that happens you'll be in an excellent position to get involved.

The question is, how do you find out about it? Make it a habit to read the local newspaper cover to cover every day. Local production of national advertising is *news* and will usually be reported in advance.

Phone the paper and ask for the reporter who wrote the story. You should be able to find out where the production crew is staying and get a name or two. Once you get through by phone, say you're a local actor and ask whether there's any work.

Most frequently, national advertising agencies cast through regional casting agencies, so you should make sure the regional agencies have your headsheet on file. A discussion of casting agencies follows later in Chapter 4.

If you're the right type, you might land a principal role, one that could earn you thousands of dollars, even if you're nonunion. There might also be extra work.

Extra work on national ads doesn't pay much, but it's great experience, and you'll learn how the big leagues do it. You'll also meet many actors from whom you can learn. Don't be afraid to pump them for trade secrets. You'll be no threat to them; they'll probably be flattered and enjoy educating you.

Extra work also has the potential to become principal work if the spot is shot under union contract. Remember that you don't have to *say* anything to be a principal, you just have to be identifiably seen, even if it's just for a second. So when the spot is edited back in the big city, if your face is visible in the final edit, the advertising agency may have to *upgrade* you from an extra to a principal. At that point, depending on where the spot plays and how long it's used, there's always the potential for lots of additional money in residual payments.

Since this is such an important point, the current Screen Actors Guild rules pertaining to upgrades are offered here. Principal performers, in addition to anyone who is seen and speaks a line or lines of dialogue, include:

1. Anyone whose face appears silent, alone in a stationary camera shot, and is identified with the product or service.
2. Anyone whose face appears silent and is identifiable and whose foreground performance demonstrates or illustrates a product or service or illustrates or reacts to the on- or off-camera narration or commercial message.
3. Anyone who is the subject of a close-up and is identifiable.

Public Service Announcements

If you watch much television you know that public service announcements (PSAs) run frequently. Is it to your advantage to seek these community-betterment opportunities? Absolutely! You'd be crazy if you didn't.

In the big city actors get paid for PSAs. Back home you probably won't. But don't worry, the rewards of doing PSAs in your home town are worth a lot more than money.

By doing them you'll gain the respect of the broadcasting community, not to mention the community at large. And you'll feel good about yourself.

Look for PSA work by telling the producers you meet that you're willing to do PSAs at no charge. If you're good, they'll take you up on your generous offer.

Chapter
FOUR
Working in Commercials

Just as you have a strategy for getting work, if you want to
keep working, you need to know how to conduct yourself
on the job and how to approach the work as a professional.
You know what you have to go through to get a commercial
job. Now you need to learn what to do when you get there.
Your objective, every time you work, is to be *asked back*.
You must deliver on a number of levels.

To prepare yourself to do that, you should understand
what goes on during a typical commercial shoot and studio
recording session.

The Shoot

A locally produced commercial shoot will be conducted in
much the same way as a national one. The differences are in
the number of people involved and the experience of the
cast and crew. Generally, the smaller productions involve
only a few people and should be far less intimidating for
you—the first-time commercial actor.

In most situations, but particularly outdoors, the shoot will
begin early in the morning. You'll be given an address and
told where to park. If it's in a city, transportation may be ar-
ranged for you. Your *call*, or arrival time, will be early
enough for you to get comfortable, get into makeup (if any)

and wardrobe, and rehearse your lines (if you're cast in a speaking part) until they are completely memorized.

It's entirely possible, perhaps even probable, that you won't see the final *copy* (the script) until you arrive; so you may have to memorize it on the spot. In most cases the shoot will be broken up into more than one shot, so you won't have to memorize the copy as a whole. But you should be prepared to if necessary. You may find it helpful to ask someone, such as the assistant director if there is one, to help you.

While you are getting ready, the technical crew—under the supervision of the director—will be setting up for the first shot. This setup, even if the technical crew is highly competent, usually takes quite a while. Lighting variations are subtle, and the final product's quality is often judged on the quality of the lighting.

To sidestep for a moment, if you watch television and compare local with national spots, you'll notice a difference in image quality. That's because national spots are most often done on film, rather than videotape. Film is preferred over videotape because of its higher resolution, and it is far more difficult to light. If your commercial is being filmed, be prepared for possibly hours of waiting while the lighting is painstakingly worked out.

Once they are ready for you to step before the camera, the director will probably ask you to stand in the shot to aid the lighting process. This may take a long time, so you might as well rehearse your lines out loud a few times. At some point during this lighting procedure the sound technician will conceal a microphone in your clothing and then ask you for an audio check. Rehearse your lines again at a natural, conversational volume.

When the lighting and audio are set, the director's attention will shift to you and any other actors who will be in the shot. You'll be told what the final product should look like, how it should be interpreted, and when and where you should walk and talk. They may show you a *storyboard*, which is a cartoon of the commercial showing all the different characters, words, shots, and actions. (*See Illustration 3.*)

You'll run through this proposed action a few times until

Illustration 3

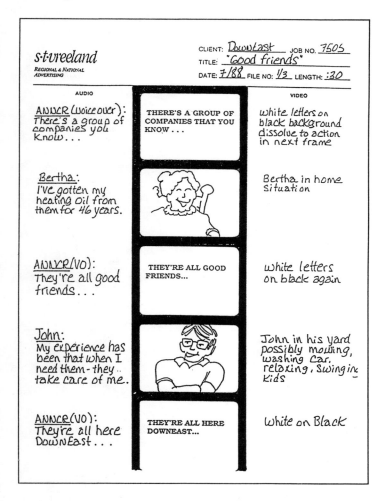

s·t·vreeland
REGIONAL & NATIONAL
ADVERTISING

CLIENT: DownEast   JOB NO. 7505
TITLE: "Good friends"
DATE: 7/88 FILE NO: 1/3 LENGTH: :30

AUDIO		VIDEO
ANNCR (voice over): There's a group of companies you know...	THERE'S A GROUP OF COMPANIES THAT YOU KNOW...	white letters on black background dissolve to action in next frame
Bertha: I've gotten my heating oil from them for 46 years.		Bertha in home situation
ANNCR (VO): They're all good friends...	THEY'RE ALL GOOD FRIENDS...	white letters on black again
John: My experience has been that when I need them - they take care of me.		John in his yard possibly mowing, washing car, relaxing, swinging kids
ANNCR (VO): They're all here DownEast...	THEY'RE ALL HERE DOWNEAST...	white on black

An example of a TV commercial storyboard (storyboard courtesy of
S.T. Vreeland Agency, Yarmouth, Maine).

(Illustration 3 continued)

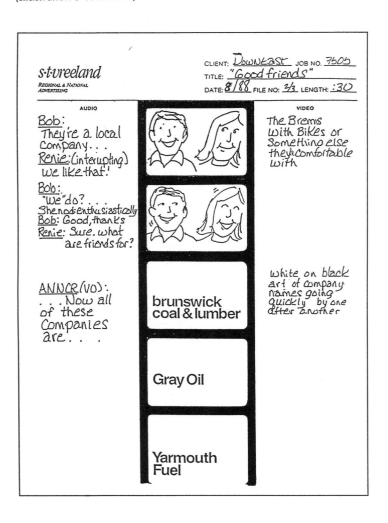

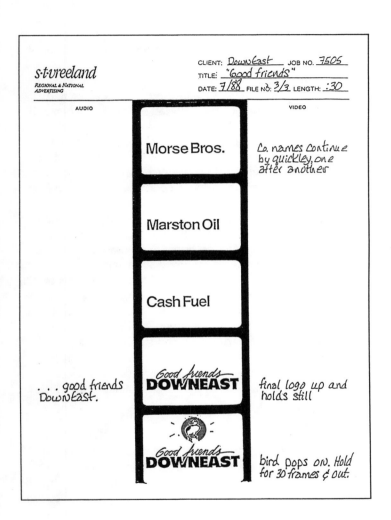

s·t·vreeland
REGIONAL & NATIONAL
ADVERTISING

CLIENT: DownEast   JOB NO. 7505
TITLE: "Good friends"
DATE: 7/88 FILE NO: 3/3 LENGTH: :30

AUDIO

VIDEO

Morse Bros.

Co. names continue
by quickley, one
after another

Marston Oil

Cash Fuel

. . . good friends
DownEast.

Good friends
DOWNEAST

final logo up and
holds still

Good friends
DOWNEAST

bird pops on. Hold
for 30 frames & out.

53

the director says, Let's put some takes on tape [film]. If ad agency staff or the client is present, they will take part in deciding when to roll the cameras.

If the spot is being filmed, you'll rehearse more and shoot fewer takes. Film is expensive. The opposite is true of videotape, so in that case plan on lots of takes.

When everyone is satisfied with the first shot (*shot* here means change of angle or subject matter), the process will be repeated for every shot the commercial requires. Your time on the job will depend on how many shots are taken and how well everyone has prepared for the shoot. In any case, for the actor, most time on a commercial shoot is of the hurry-up-and-wait variety. Bring a good book; you'll be glad you did.

After the final shot has been approved the director will say, That's a wrap. That means the technicians can pack everything up and you can go home. You may be released earlier, however, depending on when shots without you in them are scheduled. If you are scheduled to work a second day, you'll be given a call sheet.

During this entire process you'll have a unique opportunity to meet and get to know several people who might steer future work your way. Everyone on the shoot is there for a reason; and most of them, with the exception of the technicians, have had a role in the casting process. You should know who they are and what their responsibilities are.

Who's Who on the TV Commercial Set

On most commercial shoots, large and small, you'll work with agency people, clients, and production people.

The advertising agency will at minimum send an art director, but more than likely will also send the account executive and the writer. On the really small jobs all three functions may be assumed by the same person. The art director is responsible for how the final spot will look and is concerned with such things as how the set (office, store, car lot, etc.), characters, props, and product look. The writer is responsible for how the commercial sounds and how images—including you—look in relation to what's being said. Often the writer and art director confer and collaborate until both are satisfied. The account executive is there to deal with the client, making certain that everything is done to his or her satisfaction. The account executive is the client's conduit to the art director and writer, known collectively as *creative services*.

Production personnel will consist of at least one lighting/sound person and a cameraman, who may also be the director. This is probably all you'll see on the really low budget spots. On higher-budget ones there is usually a specialist for every function, including makeup.

You can expect the average crew of a shoot in a small or midsize city to consist of the client, two ad people, a director, a cameraman, a sound technician, a makeup artist, and talent. As the budget grows, so do the number of bodies around the set. If it's a union shoot, be prepared for a crowd.

Now that you know what to expect of others on the typical shoot, it's time to learn what's expected of you.

Working Professionally

Insecure, unprepared actors take too much time, which costs too much money. They're bad for morale on the set.

Think of it this way. Everyone on the shoot except the client bills by the hour. So you'd think the client would appreciate a shoot that doesn't go into overtime. You're right.

If this is your first job you probably *will* be insecure; but if you are well prepared, you'll be able to compensate for this insecurity and be ready for the pressures inherent in making a TV spot. Much of that preparation involves common sense.

Take care of yourself. This is critically important. Get plenty of sleep the night before any work or auditions, and eat a good breakfast. Commercial shoots are notorious for their length, sometimes running from ten to fourteen hours. You'll need mental and physical stamina to be as fresh at the end of the day as you were at the beginning.

On a more practical level, be prepared with appropriate *wardrobe and makeup*. Art directors usually get in touch shortly before a shoot to discuss what you should bring with you. Be sure that what you bring is spotlessly clean and properly pressed. If no one contacts you about wardrobe, don't assume that it will be provided. It's professional to call and ask. If you can't reach anyone, take along several outfits you consider suitable for your assigned character. If you don't arrive with what the job requires, at least those in charge will know you tried, and you'll know that being less than fully prepared wasn't your fault. When this happens (which is seldom), someone will be sent out to buy what is required.

Most low-budget shoots can't accommodate the expense of a makeup artist, so you should bring your makeup kit along. Know how to use it. Most women won't have a problem here, but men might. Sometimes, for a man, his natural coloring is sufficient, and makeup, other than powder to blot shine, isn't necessary. But it's always good advice to have your kit with you.

Men who don't know the basics of putting on makeup should ask a woman friend for a lesson or two. Be sure to choose a woman whose makeup is subtle, natural, and fairly conservative. That's what you'll need, too. Expertise with makeup adds to *your* value as an actor. During the shoot, ask from time to time how your makeup is doing. If you're shining up, powder down.

And while you may think it goes without saying, make it a general practice to stay out of the sun, particularly just before a shoot. It's good for your skin and will lessen your makeup requirements.

Memorization

If you have a line or lines to say in the commercial, you may receive the copy in advance. *Memorize* it well, but not to the point of rigidity, before you get to the set. Your employers will expect you not only to know all the words but also to be able to recite them spontaneously. This means you'll speak your memorized lines as though you are saying them for the first time.

You'll feel self-conscious at first, but after a while it will come more easily. People who fear memorization often don't realize how easy it really is. All it takes is discipline and the ability to concentrate on the ideas being expressed. Obviously this will be easier if you're cast in dialogue commercials in which you play a role rather than function as a spokesperson.

The important thing to understand is that if you focus on what you are saying, the ideas behind the words, and the need to communicate those ideas, memorization becomes less of a rote exercise. You will need to be flexible with the words and how you emphasize them, and may even be required to adapt quickly to script changes—yes, on-the-shoot script changes. They are part of the game, and your ability to take them in stride is critical. If you memorize the copy too well, you may lock yourself in to a stiff interpretation and be unable to handle changes or take direction.

Fear of memorization usually goes back to childhood and being asked to recite a memorized piece in front of the class. Remember how self-conscious you felt? Back then you concentrated on *remembering all the words*; and if you said each and every word, you were told you had done well. You were probably not taught that the memorizer is also a *communicator*, someone who has a message to impart. Memorizing the words is not enough; the viewer should focus on *what* you say, not on *how* you say it.

If you come to a commercial shoot with the copy well memorized or with the ability to memorize on the spot and recite with spontaneity, you will be respected as a talent who knows what he or she is doing—as someone who can handle pressure and get the job done.

In many situations you'll be asked whether you need cue cards; on higher-budget shoots, you may be asked whether you'd like to work with a teleprompter. These actor aids may occasionally be provided as a matter of course.

Teleprompters

The *teleprompter* is your true friend because it bypasses the need to memorize and all the anxiety that surrounds memorization. A teleprompter is a nifty gadget that permits actors to read lines while appearing to look directly into the viewers' eyes. The script, or copy, is reflected by mirrors onto a semireflective piece of glass angled in front of the camera lens. As the actor reads, the teleprompter operator scrolls the script to match the speaking pace. (*See Illustration 4.*)

This means that all you have to do is *read* conversationally, which is much easier, because you aren't worried about remembering the words.

If you have never used a teleprompter before your first job with one, don't worry. Just ask to practice a few times and you'll get the hang of it right away. We're dealing with a maximum of sixty seconds of copy here, not a whole book. By the time you've rehearsed several times, you'll probably have the copy virtually memorized anyway.

Again I want to stress the need for professional acting classes, which will ensure that you have teleprompter experience *before* you're on the job.

Cue Cards

Cue cards are held beside, above, or below the camera so that the talent can read his or her lines from them. (*See Illustration 5.*) Because *eye* contact with the lens (and thus the viewer) can be interrupted when cue cards are used, they are usually associated with low budgets; but if you look closely, you'll see them used in national spots every now and then.

Taking Direction

As mentioned earlier, during rehearsal and performance you'll be expected to *take direction*, which means you'll need to be and stay flexible. Directors usually ask you to read the spot in several different ways so they can get a sense of how they want the material to flow.

You'll read it at different speeds, with varying degrees of energy, and at more than one pitch level. You'll also be coached on gestures and body motions.

Most actors, particularly beginners, find that coordinating interpretation, script, and movement variations with memo-

Illustration 4

The actor looks directly at the teleprompter, which is in front of the
camera lens, to find his or her lines.

Illustration 5

Cue cards are held close to the camera so the actor can see the script with just minimal lateral *eye* movement away from the lens.

rized copy is extremely difficult. It's not easy to concentrate on words when you also have to concentrate on directorial changes. Therefore, whenever you get a change of direction and you have problems putting it all together, request a few rehearsals.

If the others on the set are experienced, they'll understand. If they don't understand, explain your problem, adding that an extra rehearsal or two will save time in the long run. They'll respond positively to that.

It's important to remember that *everyone* wants you to perform as well as you possibly can. It's in everyone's best interest to produce a quality spot.

Sometimes, though, things have a way of becoming more difficult than they have to be. Directors may be moody in response to the pressure they're under. Agency people may overstep their bounds and contradict the director's directions. Everything can become confusing when you try to perform as well as possible under these adverse, often stressful conditions. And it's very easy for the actor to misinterpret what's going on.

Quite often you will receive no direction at all except physical placement. If the director doesn't speak to you or give you specific directions, it usually means he or she is happy with what you are doing. While silence can be terrifying, it is often a compliment.

You can also help things go smoothly by observing some etiquette on the set.

First, stay out of the way of *busy* people. Actors are expected to seclude themselves while not on the set and to be ready to work immediately when called. While in seclusion, work on memorization until you feel comfortable with the spot, then read a book or something. If you want to talk, choose someone who's obviously not doing anything else.

Second, never appear to be in a bad mood or rattled in any way. You want people to claim you were easy to work with. Your attitude should always be open, friendly, and co-operative. There will be enough trouble with lighting and sound. No one appreciates a temperamental actor.

Third, try not to talk about yourself too much. Everyone knows you're an actor looking for more work, and they don't need to be reminded. You'll get better results if you let others do the talking, and even greater rewards if you appear to be interested.

Finally, never contradict the director unless asked your opinion. Let the director direct you, even if what he tells you feels wrong. Chances are if it feels wrong to you it will look wrong to him. Eventually, through trial and error, you and the director will come up with a scheme that works. Be willing to try anything suggested.

In spite of the seclusion rule, and no matter how many people are there, you probably will have plenty of time to introduce yourself to everyone. In fact, you should make it a point to do so. Lunch and breaks are a good time for this. As you move from person to person, unobtrusively jot down their names and functions so you'll remember who they are the next time you work together.

Be sure not to neglect the technicians. If they like you they'll talk you up, and that can lead to more work. One way to assure their respect, other than turning in a good performance, is to let them go ahead of you at mealtimes. This shows them you are sensitive to their need to get back to work as soon as possible. They'll appreciate the courtesy in your gesture.

At the end of the shoot be sure to ask the ad agency producer for a copy of the finished spot, and offer to pay for it. You really must have a copy of everything you've done.

The Video Demo Tape

After you've done three television commercials, it's time to invest in a video demo tape to accompany your audio tape. While the video demo tape is rarely used in casting decisions in the national arena, the local actor will find it invaluable. The smaller the city, the more importance it has, because it will often be used instead of auditions.

Your demo tape should include only professionally produced material. That's why it's pointless to put one together before you look for work. Demo tapes that are obviously amateur facsimiles project inexperience. They just don't help. So be patient and wait until you have paid jobs to put on that tape.

Again, start with at least three spots. Keep adding to your tape until it's three or four minutes long. When you have more material than you can fit into this time limit, you can edit as necessary to include only your *best* work. At that point, put your best spots at the beginning, or head, of the tape. Mix up the styles of performance if you can, so the viewer sees an actor with range and variety.

This tape isn't inexpensive to produce, but if you wait until you're working before you put it together, you'll be able to afford it. If money *is* a problem, offer some free talent work to a production house in return for some editing time. Everybody gains from this type of arrangement.

Once you have a good tape, you have proof of experience. You can either mail it, or show it during interviews. If the producer likes what he or she sees, it may be all you need to land a job. Since the tape shows what you can do, an audition may be unnecessary. If, of course, there's any question about your suitability for a given role, you'll be asked to audition. Sometimes, too, it is simply "policy" that actors must audition.

Handing out videotapes can be expensive, so ask that your tapes be sent back to you in a self-addressed, stamped envelope that you provide when you submit your tape for consideration. Also request that viewers make a copy of the tape for their future reference. If they like it, they'll want to do this anyway.

Part of your marketing strategy should be to keep a half-dozen tapes in constant circulation. The minute one comes back to you, drop it in the mail to someone else until you've exhausted your market area. When you change or update the tape, start the process again. If your tape is good, it will get you plenty of work.

For the tapes you circulate, I recommend using inexpensive VHS tapes, which, while not of broadcast quality, are suitable—and even expected—for demonstration purposes. (Obviously this marketing tactic is also important to apply to your audiotape, discussed earlier.)

The Voice Session

Commercial voice work is produced the same way locally as it is nationally. The talent stands in front of a microphone and reads in melodious tones. Right? Well, there's a little more to it than that. Let's look at a typical two-hour session.

You'll arrive at the sound studio on time. Conditions may vary greatly depending on whether it is strictly an audio studio or part of a larger operation that handles television production too.

Generally, you'll be directed to a two-room suite: a control room and a soundproof booth, separated by a large pane of glass through which the talent and director can communicate—both visually and through earphones.

You'll be met by at least one person from the ad agency, usually a producer, and one audio engineer. There could be several other people there, depending on the budget for the recording session.

Before you're asked to enter the booth, you'll receive the script. You'll also be told about the spot and how the agency wants it read. Then you'll enter the booth, shut the door behind you, settle behind the microphone, put on a pair of earphones, and wait for further instructions. You should have a pencil with you to mark up the script based on the director's comments.

At this point the audio engineer usually asks you to read the spot for "level." He needs to hear your volume level so he can adjust his equipment accordingly. His job is to make your voice sound as good as possible. He may even enter the booth to adjust the position of the mike. Once the levels are set, you will read every take at the same volume level and keep your distance from the mike consistent.

Sound easy? Well, it's deceptive. Developing the ability to deliver a technically consistent reading takes practice and experience and perhaps, if you need them, voice lessons. Some people seem to have an innate ability to read commercial copy technically well on their very first try. Most do not. If you fall into the latter category, you've got some work to do.

Your readings for level provide an opportunity for you to rehearse the spot with *your* interpretation, free of agency direction. When the levels are set, agency representatives will tell you what they thought of your rehearsals and you'll get specific line-by-line direction. Typically, you'll be told to stress specific words in a certain way, to speed up in some sections and slow down in others. In order to keep these directions (which can become confusing) straight, mark up your script with your pencil. Underline stress words. Provide yourself clues for pauses, such as . . . — , etc. (*See Illustration 6.*)

Time is critical. If the ad calls for a twenty-eight-and-a-half-second reading, that's what you're supposed to do. So expect direction such as speed it up a little; we need to shave a second off it this time.

Since the only thing that matters to anyone at an audio session is how you sound, critiques of your reading can get very picky. Don't let it faze you. Expect to read the spot many times before being released, and expect lots of direction.

If you flub up during a reading, don't worry about it. It's bound to happen, even with the most experienced readers. Just stay calm, try again, and concentrate on the ideas in the commercial. When you flub you'll usually be asked to start at the beginning and probably be given more direction. Go through the piece as directed—placing emphasis where required—without losing conversationality.

Remember that your audience cannot see you, so you must communicate fully with your voice. Every word counts in audio work, and vocal variety is one of your best tools.

Vocal variety in the audio booth is associated with pitch, volume, tempo (speed), timing, and energy. Most successful talent in this area possess a naturally pleasing and varied voice or they wouldn't work. But that doesn't mean their voices have not been developed. If you want to reach your full potential in this lucrative area of the business, plan to take voice and diction lessons and to practice regularly at home.

When the session has been completed, always ask the producer for a copy of the finished spot for your demo tape.

Illustration 6

C O P Y ~2500.9937

CLIENT _Down East_ CLIENT#/JOB# _ DRAFT#_4_

DATE _12/20/90_ JOB NAME _We're on our way Radio :60_ PROOFREAD BY ___

WRITER _Stew_ CLIENT OK/DATE __ OK TO PRODUCE ____

Sfx: Truck noise.

ANNCR: We're on our way!

We're Brunswick Coal and Lumber, your Good Friends DownEast.

Our service reaches good friends from Brunswick to Bath and

Wiscasset, Damariscotta and Boothbay Harbor. In fact, we're probably

bringing heating oil, propane and our own special brand of service to

someone in your neighborhood right now.

Our Good Friends service includes automatic delivery that gives

you 15 days to pay at our lowest cash price / with no extra charge. A

budget plan offers you Brunswick Coal & Lumber's lowest cash price,

plus earned credit on any credit balance. Our "on-call" delivery

service gives you 10 days to pay at our lowest cash price and again

there's no extra charge. Because we're a local area company naturally,

we have our own full-time service department staffed with local

people and available 24 hours a day.

For heating oil, propane and Good Friends house heating

service, call us today, we're in your neighborhood. We're

Brunswick Coal & Lumber - Your Good Friends DownEast.

Underlined words are emphasized, double underlines require strong emphasis; up-curved lines mean a rise in inflection, down-curved lines require lowering inflection; dotted lines mean speed up, hyphenated lines mean slow down; a slash means pause. You will develop your own marking system once you begin doing voice work.

Re

2500-
9936

TESTIMONIAL TV COPY REVISES 21 DEC, 1990 TAG ONLY

ANNCR (VO): Brunswick Coal & Lumber. ~~Delivering~~ *we deliver* Heating
Oil, ~~and~~ *and heating service* Propane to Brunswick, Bath, Wiscasset, *AND* Damariscotta
~~and Boothbay Harbor.~~ Your Good friends DownEast.

if the above is too long, use this abreviated version:

Brunswick Coal & Lumber. In Brunswick, Bath, Wiscasset,

Damariscotta and Boothbay Harbor. Good friends DownEast.

PRO PANE

Boothbay Harbor — Propane only — no oil
no oil
Truck

wed 26th

½ hr 8:30 - 9 - Nabo pin ty co-ord
9-9:30 - travel to deliver photo for halftone BC+L
10:45-11 - " " studio for TV/photos revise
11-11:45 - revise 2nd studio for TV revises
11:45-12 - travel to " " " "
12 -

67

You will almost always receive one or will at least be able to purchase one at the studio's standard duplication fee. As soon as you can, update your audio demo tape with your most current work. Your tape should eventually include a wide variety of spots that have all been used on the air. This helps you get even more work, because potential employers will recognize the spots they've heard; if they like the way you did them, you'll be in demand.

There's something to be said for the theory of "momentum" breeding more and more work. Up to a point, the more people you work with, the more people will want to work with you—just as long as you deliver quality. But the time may come when you'll need professional help in your marketing efforts.

After your feet are firmly on the ground, it's appropriate to wonder how you can get more work for better pay. Local and regional agents and casting agencies may be able to help you here.

Agents

If you live in or near a midsize or larger city, there may be a legitimate agent or two in residence. Many cities of eighty to one hundred thousand boast a nonunion agent. And regional hub cities, like Dallas, Miami, Houston, Denver, and Phoenix, will have both union-franchised and nonunion agents on hand.

Union-franchised agents have entered into an agreement with AFTRA or SAG in which they agree to represent union members only. This means you have to be a member of one of these unions to enter into an exclusive contract with them. But let's not get ahead of ourselves here. If you're just starting out, joining a union may not be your best strategy because there's usually more nonunion work available in all but our largest cities. And you can certainly have an agent—maybe even more than one—without joining a union and without signing an exclusive agreement.

The important point to remember, whether you're union or nonunion, is that legitimate agents, if they are motivated to work hard for you, can really help.

But, again, watch out for scams. Be wary of an agent who requires you to pay for a photo session, class, or workshop that they control before they will accept you. These people just want your money.

Legitimate agents make their money on commissions, usually 10 percent of what the actor gets paid, and try to get their actors as much money as they can. It's a process called working for the actor, not the other way around. A good agent is also honest about your prospects. If you are perceived as talented and marketable, they'll want to work for you. If they think you're wasting your time they'll reject you, not string you along.

Without actors, legitimate agents don't eat; and without agents, actors work harder to obtain jobs, and—in truth—are shut out of many opportunities. So you must get to know your area's agents (if there are any) and work with them to maximize your potential.

If there is an agent or two in your area, your best bet is to hook up with one or more as soon as you can, at least on a free-lance, nonexclusive basis.

But how do you meet these agents? The same way you work the ad agencies. Start with the yellow pages. Look under talent agencies and modeling agencies. Outside the major cities they are more often than not *one and the same.* Get them on the phone. Say you are a new actor in the area and request an appointment.

In the small cities you'll probably get an appointment right away. As the size of the cities and the number of competing actors increase, you may encounter a few obstacles. For example, busy agents often set aside specific hours each month to meet new people; others will require photos, résumés, and demo tapes before they'll meet you.

Your initial meeting with an agent is important because you will both consider the merits of a longtime association. The agent must feel that you're not only marketable, but likable. Be yourself in this meeting, and try to relax. Answer questions honestly and completely. Talk about yourself openly; the agent needs to know you and gauge your personality in order to convince others to meet you.

Don't be afraid to ask agents what you can expect from

them. You need to understand what an agent can and cannot do for you. In most instances you'll learn that the agent doesn't get you jobs, only opportunities. Those opportunities will be auditions and interviews for commercials, corporate films, print jobs, etc.

If the agent can get you enough opportunities to make it worthwhile, you may then want to enter into an exclusive contract. This means that you agree to work through that agent *only* for all your commercial work.

If there is a danger in signing with a local nonunion agent it is that you restrict yourself to that person's contacts. Then, when it's time for you to branch out of the local area, you might want to join a union and hook up with a franchised agent only to find you're tied down for the term of your contract.

Here's my best advice. If you're new to the business, try to sign with a good local agent, but limit the term of this type of legal agreement to a year. This enables you to review the arrangement annually, and when you want to move on, you won't have too long to wait.

If you choose to remain unsigned, you are free to work through agents as a free lance. The only risk here is that they might not work as hard for you as for a signed client.

So go ahead and sign if you're given a choice. And continue your personal marketing efforts as outlined in this book, always mentioning who represents you. Your agent will appreciate your efforts, and being represented will enhance your image of professionalism.

Casting Agencies

There are usually casting agencies in major cities that support a large advertising community. These organizations provide another buffer between advertising agencies and actors, and they must be considered in your plans.

In most cases casting agencies work hand in hand with agents to provide advertising agencies with plenty of talent variety. Casting agents make money from their advertising clients—not from the actor.

A casting agent gets into the act when an advertising

agency art director or producer calls and requests a "casting session" for a particular commercial. A time is set for the session, and agents are then called to submit those clients (that's you) who they feel are right for the types requested. The casting agents may also request certain actors for the session—actors they know.

The casting session is merely an audition in which actors will be videotaped reading the commercial. It shouldn't be any different from the auditions agencies sometimes hold except there may be more competition.

In cases where the casting agents work independently of talent agents, actors will be contacted directly by the casting agency.

In either case, it's important that you become known as a reliable, professional performer to all the casting agents in your region. Your pictures and résumés and demo tapes should be on hand at the casting agencies, and you should check in with them regularly.

A combination of your own marketing skills and the resources of agents and casting agencies will put you in a position to milk your area for commercial work until the ad people perceive you as overexposed or until you need to generate more income from acting than the local area can provide. The larger the city, the longer it'll take for this to happen. But when it does, you'll have to branch out. At that time you'll have to make some tough decisions, decisions about whether or not to join a union and which larger market to target.

Chapter

FIVE

Corporate and Educational Markets

Nonbroadcast corporate television is the fastest-growing work category for actors in the United States. Still called "industrials" by many, including SAG and AFTRA (which means you should still include this category as INDUSTRIAL FILMS on your résumé), corporate television now ranks second only to commercials in the number of job opportunities it creates for actors.

Corporations large and small, all over the world, increasingly use nonbroadcast television for their internal—and sometimes external—communications. Typical corporate television video subjects include demonstration tapes on how things work; informational tapes on new company policies and procedures; management and sales training tapes; tapes for clients; documentaries; and internal problem-solving tapes on topics as diverse as shoplifting, sexual harassment, stress, employee relations, and safety.

These presentations are either videotaped or (much less frequently, because of the high cost) filmed and are formatted most often as role plays or narrations. Role plays usually involve people playing the roles of employees or customers in situations designed to instruct viewers. Narrations usually feature one or two authority figures who either instruct, report company news, or sell.

Very few of these presentations will ever be broadcast into

73

people's homes over network or cable television. Corporate television, by definition, is television created for the corporation's internal use, and I'll treat it that way in this chapter.

Here are a couple of important facts that everyone interested in making money as an actor should know: one, there are corporations *in almost every city* in the United States that make films and video communications; and two, most of them pay people to appear in them. In addition to speaking parts, they need extras, people with a specific look, and people with special skills.

It's unfortunate that many people drawn to acting by visions of fame and fortune rarely think of the work available in corporations close to home. Corporate television is a sleeping giant that has provided steady income for local and regional actors for years. The volume of work available is enormous and it's definitely close to where you live.

While corporate television doesn't offer the visibility of commercials, the almost effortless income of print modeling, or the excitement and glamor of stage and film, it is no less professional and sometimes far more lucrative. The actor (not the person with a look or a special skill) needs to use all his talents here, and needs to use them well; he may even have to learn some new ones to succeed.

Getting Ready

You must understand that although commercial TV work often requires legitimate acting skills, corporate television is, for the most part, far more demanding. The average project is a ten-minute videotape rather than a thirty-second spot or a one-expression photograph.

When you consider how many takes can be shot of a thirty-second spot in an eight-hour day you realize acting ability isn't everything in commercials. Although lines must be learned and delivered honestly and expressions must be projected believably, the need for full characterization many times just isn't there, because the spot is very short and often fragmented.

Commercial actors don't need the same character-analysis techniques as stage and film actors to uncover subtle motivations. They lean more on their ability to relate to their character's immediate situation, and they don't need to look beyond that.

In corporate television you'll be expected to deliver a full characterization without throwing the shoot into overtime.

What are some of the character roles you might portray in a corporate video or film? The range is extensive, and it runs the gamut from spokesperson to high drama, soap opera style.

Some of the roles I've played over the years might give you an inkling of how wide this market is. I've played an innocent young (that was a few years ago) executive tempted by his manager to get in on some corporate graft; a computer engineer explaining how a new software product works; a sailing instructor pointing out the benefits of a certain manufacturer's sails; a mill worker faced with an unsafe working environment; a stressed-out family man whose career is disintegrating; a shipbuilder concerned about scaffolding safety; a job seeker with absolutely no job-seeking skills; and on and on. Are you beginning to get the idea?

In addition to on-camera acting, the corporate area includes lots and lots of voice work narrating videos, documentary films, slide shows, and film strips.

And don't forget our state and federal governments. They fall into this category, too.

TYPE CONSIDERATIONS

Are you a great dad type in TV spots but fail to get other kinds of roles? Are you just dying to play a bad guy? Do you get cast only as a housewife behind a mop? Could be you are frustrated with the roles you get in commercials. You may find you have a wider casting range in corporate television, where you could play anything from a spokesperson to a shoplifter to an accident victim to a manager who's about to suffer a nervous breakdown to a mechanic taking the audience through a complicated gear change.

THE CORPORATE HEADSHOT AND RÉSUMÉ

The corporate headshot and résumé should play to your corporate type. If you want spokesperson roles, you'll need a headshot that shows a business look with plenty of authority. As with commercial headshots, corporate headshots should be in black and white. (*Some examples are shown in Illustration 7.*)

Men should wear a medium to light suit (or at least a sport coat) and tie with a blue shirt, and should assume a friendly yet confident expression. No dramatic vulnerability here. Women should wear a medium to light conservative suit with a businesslike, pastel shirt—or a blazer and an appropriate blouse. For role-playing, a casual, smiling shot in semibusiness attire is fine. If you're selling a look or a special skill, your headshot and résumé should reflect that.

Use the same résumé you use for commercials, and be sure to include a category for corporate clients as soon as you have some.

Many actors feel one headshot will do for everything—commercials, print modeling, and corporate television. And they may be right. But why take the chance? It's more professional to approach each market separately. And although it costs more, it's worth it in the long run.

If you do decide to approach the corporate market at the same time you're seeking commercials, tell your professional headshot photographer to shoot at least one roll of thirty-six exposures of you in business clothing. There's certainly no need to schedule a separate photo session.

WARDROBE AND MAKEUP

The corporate actor needs a wardrobe of quality business attire. A good initial selection for men includes a navy blazer with gray slacks, a navy pinstripe suit, a gray pinstripe suit, a solid gray suit, button-down and regular-collar business shirts in blue and off-white, black and brown business shoes, and a selection of ties. Women should purchase a comparable selection. Look in business magazines to see what executives are wearing.

When investing in business attire, don't get trendy. Stick with conservative styles so you can use those outfits indefinitely.

If you're being hired for a look, a skill, or a character role, you'll be asked to bring specialized wardrobe to the shoot. In many cases this kind of wardrobe will be provided by the producer.

Most corporate video shoots don't employ a makeup artist, so you'll be expected to do your own. Put together a kit and use the techniques outlined in the commercials chapter.

DEMO TAPES

The serious actor should have demo tapes for the corporate market that include narration and dialogue. Both your audio and video demo tapes should reflect your corporate type and range and should be of high quality. This means that, at least for the videotape, you should wait until you have a few actual work samples before you put it together.

You can use copy from the audio production house where you assemble your voice demo.

Some actors advocate using a comprehensive audiotape for both commercials and corporate voice work. This is fine, but be sure to include plenty of narration and dialogue mixed in with the commercial spots. Corporate producers aren't interested in your commercial delivery unless they want you for a selling piece—which may be the case from time to time.

I use two audio demo tapes, one geared to commercials, the other to the nonbroadcast areas of corporate television and educational documentaries. The latter tape contains only narrations and dialogue.

You can use three-quarter-inch or VHS cassettes for your video demos and standard audiocassettes for your voice demos. You'll save money if you can purchase some used videocassettes.

I recommend using VHS tapes because they're less costly to buy and mail. Reusing tapes may sound unprofessional, but by removing the old labels and replacing them with new ones you'll get around that. New labels will make your used tapes appear as good as new. You can find used tapes at video production houses.

Putting a videotape together is an expensive proposition, and there's no way around it. The tapes themselves, even

Illustration 7

Pete Kovner

Pat Dugan

These typical "corporate" headshots project feelings of assertiveness, confidence, and leadership ability. Note the business attire each actor has chosen.

Ted Norton

Photo by Lynn McCann

David Berti

Photo by Lynn McCann

Bertha Leverone

Cope Murray

Photo by Linda Holt

Cope Murray

used ones, are costly, and you will need several duplicates to mail around. It takes time to edit a quality demo tape, and the cost of editing time can be very high. It's reasonable to expect that in the business of acting for business, actors may spend hundreds of dollars producing a demo tape that says "quality" and creates a good impression.

Unless you limit yourself to spokesperson roles, you should compile a tape that includes several selections in three or four minutes. Let's say you choose two spokesperson, one voice-over, and three role-playing pieces. This allows for plenty of variety. Try to mix the viewing order so that no two spots of a single category appear back to back, and try to start the tape with a piece in which you come on camera and introduce yourself.

This takes time and money, but will be well worth both. One way to save money is to offer a production company your acting services in return for their help in producing your demo. Many production companies like such arrangements.

BUSINESS CARDS

Business cards are essential for the corporate video actor. Their design should be understated, and your skills should be mentioned. For example, if you see yourself as a spokesperson, the card should say so. A typical card might look like this:

WILLIAM PAUL STEELE

Actor   Narrator   Spokesman

Telephone (123) 456-7890

115 Smith Road
Anywhere, USA

This card says you are available for role-playing, voice narration, and on-camera spokesman roles. If it's well designed (don't use fancy logos), you can hand it out with confidence. Many actors hand out their business cards in Rolodex as well as standard format. If you're a union member, include your affiliations on your card.

Looking for Corporate Work

Where are those corporate jobs? Probably closer than you think.

You'll need to learn which companies within a reasonable travel distance (for me it's two and a half hours) produce videos and which production houses help them do it. You'll need to keep an eye on audition advertisements in your local paper. And you'll also need to meet all the independent producers and directors in your market, because they're the ones who have the jobs you want. So do you break out the yellow pages? You could, but that's a labor-intensive process. Why not join the International Television Association (ITVA) instead?

THE INTERNATIONAL TELEVISION ASSOCIATION

The International Television Association (ITVA) is the organization of choice for video professionals nationwide because it offers many helpful services. While actors do not play an essential role in the framework of the ITVA's intent, they may join and get involved. The ITVA is the best way to meet and be met by corporate producers who need actors. (If you're marketing a look or skills, there's no need to join.)

The ITVA works for actors for a number of reasons. First, it boasts a huge membership from almost every corporate video department or related business in the United States. Second, college and university television production personnel choose the ITVA as their professional organization. Third, its membership ranks are teeming with independent producers and directors. Fourth, the ITVA provides an annual membership directory to all members. And fifth, there is probably a chapter within a reasonable commuting distance of where you live.

The video professional, just like any other professional, should belong to a national association designed to keep its members current and provide opportunities for cross-fertilization. The ITVA does just that. Each year members can go to its national convention, make use of the organization's job-search services, share ideas with local chapter members each month, and use the national membership directory to locate geographically distant members.

The ITVA also puts out a number of helpful publications and holds an annual video contest in which awards for excellence in video production are given. Many individual chapters give their own awards in locally run contests. All of this career-supporting activity, and the fact that there is little competition from other video organizations, means that the ITVA is a *must* for any video professional who wants to stay on top of his or her field. It also means the ITVA is a must for you.

Joining the ITVA is easy. Just write ITVA, 6311 North O'Connor Road, LB 51, Irving, Texas 75039 to request a membership application and the name and telephone number of the chapter president nearest you. If you want to speed things up, phone the national office at (214) 869–1112.

As soon as you can, call the chapter president and request a meeting schedule. Then go to the meetings and circulate. You *can* do this before you join, but joining is essential to receive those vital membership lists.

Usually ITVA meetings consist of a social hour followed by a business meeting and a presentation or two by video specialists and vendors. You'll meet people who will be important to you later by talking with them during the social hour. Try to be very casual about it. This is not the time to sell yourself; in fact, *producers and directors might resent your advances at this time.* Efforts to market yourself aggressively should come later. The social hour is a time to be polite, interested, and interesting. It's also a good time to ask people you think can help you for their business cards. When you do, they'll probably ask you for yours.

Direct self-selling will be easier after you've met the same people several times. They'll know you when you call and may be receptive to evaluating your demo materials. If you've taken the time to circulate at these meetings, you'll improve your likelihood of getting work.

Corporate video people tend to wary of actor/ITVA members who appear too hungry. Bide your time; just be there and gradually get to know who's who.

As any chapter president will tell you, many ITVA members are pretty irregular in their meeting attendance; so you'll have to make some cold calls. Use your membership directory as a phone book. It's certainly easier than using the yellow pages.

THE ITVA ANNUAL MEMBERSHIP DIRECTORY

Every year each member receives an updated directory. If you use this directory to its full potential, you may never need to haul out the phone book again! The directory contains the name, title, company affiliation, company address, and phone number of every member—listed by chapter. All you have to do is turn to your chapter's listing, and you're ready to pick up the phone or get out a mailing.

AGENTS AND CASTING AGENCIES

The same agents and casting agencies discussed in Chapter 4 are no doubt plugged in to corporate television. In fact, the larger your metropolitan area, the more area corporations will use the services of agents and casting agencies. In the New England region, for example, many corporations near Boston, Hartford, and Providence routinely use casting agencies to find talent if they cannot cast their presentations from their own talent files. (Be aware, though, that union membership may be necessary to compete effectively in some large cities.)

In the smaller cities, however, like Portsmouth, New Hampshire, or Portland, Maine, corporate producers are less likely to go to the expense of hiring these professional talent scouts and they are more likely to use nonunion talent.

In any case, you should connect with the agents and casting agencies in your area to supplement your individual marketing efforts.

Educational Markets

Educational videotapes, slide shows, and audiotapes are created with *teaching* in mind. They are produced—in much the same way as corporate projects—at educational radio and television stations, colleges and universities, and professional production studios.

Most colleges and universities have a communications department that offers courses in mass media and television and radio production. State universities usually carry National Public Radio (NPR) and Public Broadcasting System (PBS) television broadcasts and are licensed by the Federal Communications Commission to produce local broadcasts. These same colleges and universities often hook into local cable television networks for additional production opportunities. They may even offer courses on the air.

All but the smallest colleges and university branches seem to have a campus radio station, but many of the jobs there have to go to students. If you're just starting out and need training and experience, you could kill two birds with one stone by enrolling in some courses to sharpen your skills and offering to work for the station as well. You might not get a prime on-air shift right away, but if you have a good voice and pay your dues by taking on some nonair duties, you might get a chance to show your stuff.

By volunteering your services to the campus radio station you'll be on the spot for those paid jobs when they occur. On-air radio work is excellent training for those future voice-over jobs. You'll become comfortable with the mike and get plenty of feedback for improvement.

The college or university near you is probably geared toward more radio and television production than you realize; it's an opportunity in your own backyard.

If your college or university wants to make a student recruitment video, they'll need a good voice-over or on-camera spokesperson. Did you know that many medical schools offer doctor recertification courses via audiotape? Those courses are almost always professionally narrated. Just think about it—the market is already vast, and it's *growing*.

If the educational production people you need to meet aren't members of the ITVA, you'll need to get through to them directly. Each station will have a production manager, who you should be sure has your headshot, résumé, and demo tapes on hand. Use your corporate demos here. These stations routinely produce documentaries and hire voice people to do station breaks. They also (on occasion) have job openings for full-time on-air personalities to host talk shows, present the news, and anchor music programs.

One way to meet college and university producers is to take a course in television production. This way you'll learn the technical aspects of video production, and you'll set up a direct line to the school's production personnel. Volunteer your services as an actor; it's a good way to get started. If you're good, you'll get your foot or maybe your whole body in the door.

The educational market offers you an enormous number of opportunities, almost all with built-in credibility. Being associated with education can't help but reflect positively on you.

I strongly recommend that anyone wishing to pursue a local, state, and regional acting career spend some time cultivating this market. Even if you are successful in commercials and corporate video, appearing in the educational arena will afford you real respect in your home town.

Working in the Corporate and Educational Arenas

Your work habits will make or break you here just as they will in any other acting area. Your objective is to be asked back and recommended to others.

SCRIPT STUDY

If you're hired for a speaking part, studying your script is very important because it will help you work efficiently during the shoot. In terms of *memorization*, you'll need to know your lines well enough to get through the script, but not so well that you're tied to a specific interpretation of the words. Remember the discussion of commercials? The important thing to understand about memorization is that you must be flexible enough to take direction and to concentrate on the idea *behind* the words.

This needs some clarification. In the theatre, actors usually receive their scripts at the first rehearsal, which is traditionally a read-through and some degree of analysis with the director. Only after interpretive decisions have been made does the actor begin to memorize lines. As rehearsals progress over a typical four-week span, lines, interpretation, movement, and character are all learned at the same time—gradually.

Not so in film and video. Here you are expected to arrive on the set ready to go. If you show up with everything learned so tightly that you're inflexible about taking direction, you'll have a rough time. It's only when you're on the set that the director will suggest movements and give you props to handle; you'll have to learn those things on the spot and coordinate them with your lines.

Line-memorization technique for video and film is unique. You must train yourself to memorize only so far, and no further. Know the words cold, but be able to accommodate changes in both script and interpretation.

TELEPROMPTERS

The teleprompter is used extensively in video to save actors—and producers—the few days' time memorization requires.

Corporate producers usually operate under a strict budget and don't want to risk dealing with actors who don't know their lines. The teleprompter is therefore almost always used for on-camera narrations and also quite frequently for scripted role-playing scenes.

In the latter case, television screens are placed over the shoulders of the actors engaging in conversation. The script is televised onto those screens and scrolled along at the conversational pace by the teleprompter operator. All the actors need do is read their lines as they pop up on the screen. (*See Illustration 8.*)

You'll need to remember not to shift your eye contact from the teleprompter to the actor or actors with whom you're playing the scene because this type of eye movement tips off the viewer that a teleprompter is being used. Never take your eyes off the teleprompter. As the other actor says the lines, react as though you are looking directly into his (or her) eyes. This way you won't appear to be reading.

The on-camera narrator or spokesperson, too, should prepare for the teleprompter. Unlike the short format of television commercials, two- to three-minute narrative scenes are common in corporate and educational video. That's a lot of copy. If you must read for that long a period from a teleprompter, you ought to know what you're reading and where the emphasis should be. Practice reading those long passages out loud so things will go smoothly when you're in front of the camera.

Always rehearse out loud when working on a script at home. (*Illustration 9 is an example of a page from a corporate video script.*) Reading out loud should be part of any actor's routine. This is particularly true if you want to be a spokesperson. Your ability to read copy flawlessly will keep you working and make auditions and working with teleprompters easy. So remember the advice you were given in Chapter 1. Make reading aloud at home a part of your *everyday* preparation.

When preparing for a job on which you will be using a teleprompter your objective will be to become sufficiently familiar with your lines so you won't muddle through a cold reading and waste studio time. You should read with spontaneity.

The director will be on hand in both narrative and role-playing situations to help you interpret lines and character, but the directorial focus won't be entirely on you. It will also be concentrated on lighting and how the camera shots are framed, so you'll need to learn fast when it comes to taking direction. This will be easy if you've done your homework.

Illustration 8

In this role-playing situation Harriet Dawkins finds her lines on the
teleprompter, which she sees over Tom Power's left shoulder.

Illustration 9

A page from a corporate video script prepared by the Key
Corporation.

Remember, you want to be asked back. Unprepared actors are rarely hired a second time.

THE EARPROMPTER

One way to help ensure that you're asked back is to circumvent both memorization and the teleprompter. How do you do that? With the earprompter, of course.

The earprompter is a relatively new prompting system that makes actors', producers', and directors' jobs much easier. It's a tiny earpiece with a built-in receiver, a neck loop, and a microcassette recorder. The earprompter is "personal" equipment and is (as a rule) owned by the actor rather than supplied by the studio.

The earprompter simplifies everything about shooting. There's no need to memorize and/or use a teleprompter; script changes can be assimilated in a matter of seconds; and camera angles can be set up without regard for whether the actor can see the teleprompter.

Here's how it works. The neck loop is hidden under the actor's shirt or blouse and is connected to the microcassette recorder, which is then placed in a rear hip pocket or taped to the back of the actor's outfit, completely out of sight. (*See Illustration 10.*)

Once everything is in place, the actor reads the section of script to be taped into the microcassette recorder, at the pace the director wants. The recorder is then rewound. When the actor presses the play switch, the recorded script is broadcast from the microcassette recorder into the earpiece. The actor then speaks the same words he or she hears, at a two- or three-word delay, with complete freedom of eye contact and movement. The earprompter is appropriate for both dialogue and narration situations.

That's right, dialogue. If you record your speeches *and* your cues, you can use the earprompter in dialogue situations by using a pause switch. But be sure to purchase a tape recorder that has a remote jack. This jack allows you to use a handheld, body-taped, or foot-operated pause switch. Since the earprompter is quite popular these days, you should be able to find an actor in your region who's using one and who can advise you.

Illustration 10

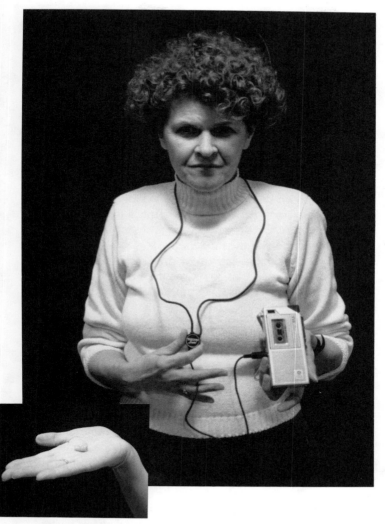

Caroline Hendry wears a neck loop that is plugged into a
microcassette recorder. On a shoot, the neck loop would be worn
under her clothing and the tape recorder concealed in a pocket. The
wireless earprompter (inset) goes in her ear.

And that's it. A remarkable piece of applied technology that saves time and money. If you're good with the earprompter, you'll get plenty of work. But don't run out and invest in one without finding out whether you can use it well; not everyone can.

To test whether the earprompter is right for you, record some copy on a cassette tape and play it back using headphones. Try to speak along with the recording without getting confused. Practice the same piece several times to get comfortable. You'll know right away whether or not you take to it.

One way to check yourself is to record your practice session on still *another* recorder and play back the "earprompted" performance. If it sounds natural to you, you'll know you're using the device properly. Check Appendix C for the names and addresses of hearing-aid companies who make *wireless* earprompter systems. They'll tell you how much a system will cost and give you the name of a hearing-aid specialist who can fit you for one.

If you want a manual system (some actors find the audio quality is better), one that has wire and a hollow tube running from the recorder to the earpiece, ask a hearing-aid company near you to rig one up. Tell them you want a custom "behind the ear" ear mold with a long tubing that will fit under your suit coat collar, shirt, or blouse, connected to a receiver adapter and a button receiver, with a cord going from the button receiver to an earphone plug that fits your tape recorder's output (listening) jack. (*See Illustration 11.*)

Make certain they understand the impedance match (the balance of the loudness of the sound coming from the tape recorder to the ear mold) that is necessary. In other words, the button receiver has to have the same impedance as the recorder's output. It's a good idea to bring your tape recorder with you. (Don't worry. If you tell them all this as written, they'll know what to do!)

The manual system is adequate for most situations, although it's not as flexible as the wireless in allowing for body movement and concealment. But it's less expensive.

I take both a wireless and manual system whenever I go on a shoot. While I prefer the manual for audio clarity, I

Illustration 11

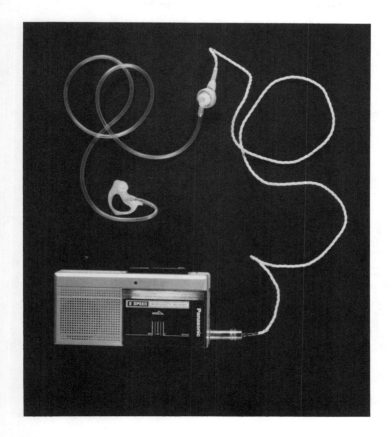

With the manual earprompter, a custom "behind the ear" ear mold is connected by a hollow tubing to a button receiver, which is connected by a wire to an earphone jack, which plugs into your tape recorder.

bring the wireless along in case the director must shoot me from an angle that would expose the cord. Whichever you choose, it's a good idea to get two of everything—two earprompters, two neck loops, two tape recorders, two sets of batteries, and so on. If your equipment fails during a shoot, your backups will bail you out.

Producers who have worked with earprompter-proficient actors love the system because it saves them money and time. They don't have to rent a teleprompter and hire someone to operate it. They also save the time it takes for an actor to rehearse coordinating lines with movement and business.

Directors love the earprompter because it eliminates the lateral eye movement associated with teleprompters, and because it enables the actor to make eye contact with his environment. They particularly like the system on remote location shoots where it's impossible to use a teleprompter. If you decide to make a serious career push in corporate television, an earprompter may give you a leg up on the competition. While the teleprompter is still used extensively in the commercial and corporate arenas, earprompter-proficient actors have a definite advantage because they can offer producers and directors more for their money.

Earprompters are also wonderful for actors who do live trade shows and must memorize somewhat lengthy, often highly technical information. Since trade show work comes primarily out of the corporate market it is mentioned here. However, since it's usually given to highly seasoned, union actors, we won't examine it in detail. If this kind of work interests you, discuss it with your agent and casting agency contacts.

CUE CARDS

Cue cards are found only occasionally in today's corporate and educational markets and are used as an alternative to teleprompters and earprompters in situations where, for budgetary or other reasons, they are the best prompting system available.

DICTIONARIES

Corporate video can be quite technical, so you may want to have some dictionaries on hand to help with those pronunciations. This is particularly true if you run into any medical narrations or have to play a doctor. So go to a good book store and pick up a copy of *Webster's Collegiate Dictionary* and *Gould Medical Dictionary* or *Dorland's Illustrated Medical Dictionary* as a start. You'll use them over and over as you get more work.

The Corporate/Educational Shoot

Let's look at what you might expect at a generic corporate/ educational shoot. This time you're in a role-playing situation in a management training video. The shoot is on location in the corporation's home office.

Remember, the company—let's say this is an insurance company—is making this video for itself. Since most insurance companies are sizable, the crew is in-house—probably from the audiovisual resources department, or a department with a similar name.

The shoot starts at nine, and is scheduled to last all day, with wrap time set for five. Yes, nine to five. This *is* corporate America. But it doesn't always work out that way.

When you arrive, you're introduced to everyone working on the project. Since the video is being produced in the home office, there are only a few people working on the crew. There's a camera operator who's also acting as the director. Someone else is running the tape deck and audio equipment and a lighting specialist is on hand. (In some situations all these functions may be taken on by the same person. If so, things may take somewhat longer.)

You're introduced to the other actor, of course. Since this is your first corporate shoot, she's probably more experienced and will be able to teach you a great deal in a hurry. You explain that you're a newcomer and ask her to bear with you and run some lines.

Lines? Yes, you have a speaking part, and this shoot's not teleprompted. It would be if it were just you as a spokesperson, but since it's dialogue and on location, two teleprompters would be needed, and the company doesn't want to spring for the extra cost. Even though you haven't yet invested in an earprompter, you have no problem since you received your script a week ago and have had a chance to memorize it.

You and the other actor have time to rehearse your lines together while you put on makeup. (You can expect to do your own makeup for most of these corporate shoots. If you're at all shaky about this, ask your acting partner for help.)

Somewhere along the line you dress for the shoot. You'll probably put on the plain gray suit with blue shirt (or blouse) and red tie (or kerchief). Then, with makeup and wardrobe on and lines rehearsed you're asked to "step into the shot" for final lighting adjustments.

This process takes a while, so you suggest to your more experienced and confident partner that you continue running lines. As you rehearse, you use your environment (the set) and try to find believable things to do with your hands.

Where are you? In a business setting, no doubt—probably at a desk or conference table that is strategically littered with papers, clipboards, file folders, and writing instruments. These things are there to authenticate the scene and your actions—so use them whenever it seems appropriate.

When the lighting's set, the director asks you to rehearse the scene so that camera moves and angles can be worked out. Since this is a location shoot, only one camera is being used. That means that every time the camera angle is changed the action stops and you have to do the scene again from the new angle.

(Usually the scene will first be shot from a wide angle to include both the actors and the entire set, then close-ups will be shot of each actor. You'll have to perform the scene successfully at least three times in its entirety. Sometimes the scene will be done in segments, however, easing the pressure on memorization. When an actor makes a mistake in dialogue shoots, the director often picks the action up at a point just before the mistake was made rather than repeat the entire scene. This makes it easier on you in terms of memorization, but more difficult in terms of character. You must be prepared to stop and start without losing your character's believability.)

After several takes from every angle, enough to give the director plenty of choices in the editing room, the shoot wraps. After you remove your makeup and get out of wardrobe, you offer to help clear the set. (This last cooperative touch might just land you another job.)

Again, this question of whether or not to help clear the set has come up. The shoot I've just described is definitely *non-union*. The technicians are all employees of the company and are not worried about protecting their "rice bowl." They just want to get home as early as possible. If a little help from you can speed things up, your offer will be appreciated in this situation. If the crew is union, it's best not to make this kind of offer.

Spokesperson shoots, even location ones, are almost always teleprompted unless you have an "ear." All you'll do is read the script and act natural in front of the camera. When you make a mistake in this format, the director has the same options as he does in dialogue scenes. You'll either repeat the entire scene until you get it right, or you'll pick it up from just before the flub. Either way, expect to do many takes from many angles.

The Voice Session

Corporate and educational voice work is executed in much the same manner as commercial voice work. The script is recorded in a studio; you work with a producer and an audio engineer. Unless the corporation or educational station has its own sound studio, recording takes place at a production studio—the same one at which you might also tape commercials.

There are differences between commercial and corporate/educational voice sessions, however. Commercial copy must be read according to an exact time frame, but corporate/educational copy doesn't usually carry time restrictions. It isn't usually as upbeat, either. Most of it will center on instructional material designed for audiocassettes or as a voice-over for slides, filmed documentaries, or videotapes. Therefore the material will be more straightforward. (*See Illustration 12.*)

Illustration 12

#26 CALENDER UNWIND SYSTEM SAFETY TRAINING VIDEO SCRIPT   page 1

     Video   Audio

- -

                                 THE NUMBER 26 CALENDER UNWIND SPOOL HANDLING SYSTEM ON R-15 MACHINE IS A SELF-CONTAINED, BUT COMPLEX PIECE OF EQUIPMENT. IT IS DESIGNED TO UNWIND THE COATED ROLLS COMING OFF OF R-15 AND FEED THE PAPER INTO THE SUPERCALENDER SECTION.

AS WITH ALL MACHINERY IN THE MILL, YOU MUST BE PROPERLY TRAINED AND FULLY QUALIFIED TO OPERATE 26 UNWINDER.

A TRAINED OPERATOR WILL TEACH YOU HOW TO ACTUALLY RUN THE SYSTEM. HOWEVER, DURING THE NEXT FEW MINUTES, WE WILL REVIEW THE SAFE OPERATION OF 26 UNWIND SYSTEM AND HIGHLIGHT POTENTIAL HAZARDS IN THE SYSTEM THAT YOU MAY ENCOUNTER.

An example of narrative copy of the type you might encounter in corporate/educational voice work (copy courtesy of Cornerstone Communications).

Video	Audio

- -

LET'S BEGIN BY TAKING A MOMENT
TO WATCH A COMPLETE OPERATING
CYCLE, FROM REMOVAL OF AN
EMPTY SPOOL TO THE PROPER
LOADING OF A NEW ROLL.

MUSIC BRIDGE WHILE OPERATION
IS SEEN.

IT IS ALWAYS IMPORTANT TO BE
FAMILIAR WITH EQUIPMENT THAT
YOU ARE OPERATING. BUT
REMEMBER, AWARENESS AND COMMON
SENSE ARE REALLY YOUR BEST
PROTECTION.

BRIEF MUSIC BRIDGE TO RECAP.

For the purposes of this discussion let's put you in a studio reading a thirty-minute instructional narration.

Thirty minutes of copy is a long narration; and since you're being paid by the hour, your ability to read quickly and well determines whether you'll be asked back.

You're asked to read the entire document from beginning to end rather than scene by scene. You stop only for direction or when you make a mistake—which you do. In fact, you probably make several. But don't worry, even the most experienced readers make mistakes, and producers expect them to.

You'll be expected to maintain a consistent pace and energy level and to stress key words. Much of the direction you receive will be in these areas, and if you're a beginner, expect plenty.

An experienced narrator will be able to cruise through a thirty-minute script in an hour or less. A beginner may take twice as long. Again, don't worry. A two-hour session for thirty minutes of copy is acceptable.

Only if you are thoroughly prepared will you be able to overcome the nervousness that's part of that first time in the recording booth. Ask for the script in advance and work with it.

You may not be able to get the script before the session, but you should try. If you must read it cold, ask for some time to look it over before recording begins. As you become more and more experienced you'll be able to handle cold readings with confidence. In fact, many experienced narrators pride themselves on their ability to read cold.

When you reach the point of being able to walk into a booth with copy you've never laid eyes on and read it with perfect pace and emphasis and few mistakes, you've arrived. By that time you should be very busy; it takes substantial experience to get to this point.

Once You're Established

Satisfactorily completing several corporate and educational on-camera and voice-over jobs will help you establish regular clients who give you regular work. However, once you're

perceived by a client as being overexposed, you'll probably
be dropped from that client's talent pool for a while.

The actor who understands this natural course of events
makes sure to keep developing new clients to take the place
of the old ones. He keeps updating his résumé and demo
tape and calling on new prospects. The successful actor
never stops marketing herself.

Remember that people change jobs frequently in both the
corporate and educational markets; the producer who hired
you for company X, which now sees you as overexposed,
may have plenty of work for you at company Y—if you've
maintained the contact. Stay in touch with everyone you've
worked for. You have to, because others will. Never forget
that this business is very competitive.

What to Charge

Until you're established you'll have to charge minimum rates
to compete. What are minimum rates? Again I recommend
seeking the advice of an experienced actor about the acceptable scale in your region. Many corporations are accustomed
to hiring both union and nonunion talent and are willing to
pay union minimums to everyone. But, since established
minimums fluctuate from region to region and company to
company, you'll have to do a little investigating before you
seek corporate or educational work. Ask some of your instructors or check with the theatre department of a college or
university near you for the names of successful local actors.
These actors will know what you should charge.

Once you're recognized as a reliable, experienced professional you won't have any difficulty raising your rates above
established minimums.

But here's a warning. If you're nonunion, it's always best
to negotiate financial matters *up front*, including whether or
not you can expect to be paid for overtime. One of the most
unpleasant shoots I've ever experienced occurred when I
failed to establish an overtime provision before starting work.
I had agreed to work for $300 a day for three days, a high
rate back in the mid-seventies. But by the end of the first
fourteen-hour day I was feeling a little abused. So I asked

the producer what she thought would be fair to charge for overtime.

"Overtime?" she said. "There's no overtime on this shoot, Bill. You knew that."

Well, I hadn't known that. But I should have. By the end of that three-day shoot I had logged forty-two hours in front of the camera and been paid for twenty-four. My attitude the last two days of the shoot was less than optimum and so was my performance. The sad thing is it could have all been avoided with just a few up-front questions. Remember, it's important for you to know what you're getting into.

Chapter
SIX

Theatre and Movies

If Hollywood is the Mecca for movies, Broadway's the center for stage, right? Not necessarily. Broadway certainly *is* the center for *commercial* theatre, but is it the pinnacle for *artistic* theatre as well? Many knowledgeable people feel that it's in our regional theatres, such as the Alley Theatre in Houston, Texas; the American Repertory Theatre in Cambridge, Massachusetts; or the Trinity Repertory Company in Providence, Rhode Island, that our most important drama is being produced. And they're right. The reason is economics.

Broadway is ruled by the unions and the high cost of facility rental. It costs a small fortune to stage even a simple, one-set, small-cast drama. And musicals? Perish the thought. There is so much money involved that box office draw becomes the producer's prime consideration. That's why Broadway always offers a greater proportion of musicals and situation comedy than anything else. Musicals and situation comedy have broad appeal, whereas serious and experimental plays have limited appeal.

Local and regional theatres, on the other hand, operate with fewer box office demands. The good ones get by on a combination of revenue sources. Box office provides approximately 40 percent. The rest is gathered from patrons and donors, as well as state and federal arts commissions.

Regional and local producers can take more risks and put

on more plays that are considered artistic. So popular are local and regional professional theatres, in fact, that no self-respecting small or midsize city today wants to be without one. Why? People who go to the theatre spend money, and not just on theatre.

Therefore, there is a nationwide trend in support of local and regional theatre. New theatres pop up all the time, and there's probably one or more near you now. And you'll want to get involved, particularly if you are career-oriented and want to take advantage of all the acting opportunities available.

What You'll Need

Most of the regional actors with whom I work and compete agree that on the local and regional levels, marketing tools for the commercial, corporate, and theatrical arenas can be combined. Your commercial headshot, if it projects your personality and appearance in a natural way, should serve you well here. Your résumé, if you are actively going to pursue theatre work, should contain a section of theatrical roles played, the theatres in which you've performed, and perhaps the directors with whom you've worked. Theatrical training might also be highlighted. Look at the sample resumes in Chapter 2 for examples of how you can include your theatre work on your résumé.

Of course you'll also need things like postcards with your picture on them to use as friendly reminders, a good appointment book to keep yourself organized, and all the other commonsense work aids outlined in Chapter 2. With everything you need in hand you'll be ready to look for theatre work.

Looking for Theatre Work

It's very important to understand that most dinner theatres, summer theatres, small local repertory theatres, and even many regional theatres outside the major U.S. cities are non-Equity (the Actors' Equity Association—AEA—is the stage actors' union, so "non-Equity" means nonunion). And even when a regional theatre *is* associated with Actors' Equity (a trend that is accelerating), an arrangement is often made whereby only a percentage of the actors have to be Equity, sometimes as few as two or three. This means that many roles that used to be cast in New York or regional Equity auditions are now available for the local, non-Equity actor who can work for less money with no union restrictions. These roles are often cast in open auditions advertised locally.

(If you are a SAG or an AFTRA member, you should check with your regional office to see whether you are eligible to accept nonunion jobs at Equity theatres. Since AFTRA, SAG, and AEA are closely aligned, you may not be permitted to take nonunion roles at Equity theatres or at theatres Equity is trying to organize if you are a member of AFTRA or SAG.)

THE THEATRICAL AUDITION

Theatrical auditions differ greatly from commercial or corporate television auditions. For the most part they are held live, in a theatre, for the directors and producers; they're rarely videotaped. In addition, actors are expected to present prepared monologues (a monologue is a dramatic soliloquy or a dramatic sketch performed by a solo actor) before being asked to read scenes from a play.

In the case of a prepared audition, you'll be told what to prepare. Usually a short—two minutes—presentation of two contrasting pieces will do the trick. Your selections should play to your ability, age range, and type and should reveal your strengths. At least one should be a contemporary, realistic character—unless you're reading for a Shakespearian company, of course.

Choose your material carefully. You want to work with monologues that will involve you and keep you involved through repeated auditions. It's also important to work with material that won't turn off your prospective employers.

Involvement is a key word in the audition process. Directors want to hire actors who can connect with their characters internally, and your audition should show that ability. So choose monologues that help you reveal true emotion as you perform.

There are many monologue collections available today to help you, but beware. They sell very well, so you know there are thousands of actors using those same monologues. And you don't want to choose the ones directors are sick of.

Here's a safe suggestion that's worked for several successful actors I know: choose monologues from playwrights recognized as challenging and great. Arthur Miller, Edward Albee, Eugene O'Neill, Clifford Odets, and Tennessee Williams fall into this category. So do Chekhov, Brecht, and O'Casey, as well as Shepard, Ayckbourn, and Mamet. Of course there are more, many more.

Check with a college or university theatre department for advice here. Better yet, if you haven't already done so, enroll in a course that focuses on theatrical auditions. You'll be exposed to lots of useful material and personal suggestions.

In any case, it makes sense to prepare your audition pieces long before you will actually use them and to prepare several, including songs if you sing, to be ready for any situation.

You'll know you were successful with your monologue if the director asks you to read from a play. All your practice reading aloud will start to pay off here, but there's a catch. When auditioning for plays, as opposed to commercials or corporate videos, reading with machinelike accuracy and without hesitation can be a negative. Sure, the director will be impressed if you can pick up a script you've never seen before and read it flawlessly, but that's not a quality you're being considered for.

People, including full-blown characters in plays, do not communicate flawlessly in real life. They pause, they hesitate, and they reveal what they mean in subtle ways that go way beyond the words they choose to say. So when you audition for plays, you need to consider this and not get trapped by your ability to read with precision.

BIT PARTS

Walk-on roles and bit parts pay, too, if they're being cast by large professional theatres; and the experience requirements and competition for them are not as great as they are for major roles. Try to break into your local regional theatre as a bit player as early as you can. The sooner you get in, the shorter the road to major roles. You can add bit-part work to your acting résumé, and it can help fill in the financial gaps and give you credibility as you seek other acting opportunities in your home town.

When you're ready, contact the artistic directors of the local and regional theatres near you. Provide them with your headshot and résumé and explain that you are interested in bit parts as well as larger roles. If you are seen as a desirable type for upcoming plays, you may get work. The credits will look great when you decide to branch out.

It might also be advisable, if you can afford the time, to work in nonunion theatres for free. There are many small professional theatres that pay only a small percentage of their personnel, yet have the reputation of doing quality work. There will be times when a strong credit on your résumé may be more important to you than the small salary bit parts usually generate. So don't rule out working for free in professional theatre. The experience alone can help you tremendously as you move up the theatrical ladder.

OTHER MARKETS

There are other theatrical avenues for making money in your home town.

College and community theatre directors are at the mercy of those who try out for their plays. If good people show up they're overjoyed. If the good people stay home, they're devastated and run to the phone. The good actors will be contacted, old favors will be cashed in, and—occasionally—financial deals will be struck. Many community and college theatres regularly budget contingency funds for hiring experienced and reliable talent to fill in casting gaps. If you think you fill that bill, you should let everyone in your area know you're available.

Doing so is easy. Call all the community and college theatres in your area for a mailing address and a list of directors. Also, request the dates and times of any upcoming open auditions. Then, mail each director on your list a cover letter and a copy of your headshot and résumé and show up at open auditions.

While auditioning for a specific amateur production may not be appropriate at this stage in your effort to establish a career, open auditions are a good time to meet directors and explain how you can help them if they need to broaden their talent base.

If you are an older actor, you may be particularly attractive to college directors, who often avoid plays with difficult, mature roles. Your availability might just allow a college director to choose a play that wouldn't ordinarily be produced.

Don't rule out working in college or community theatre for free if you need the experience or if you need some exposure in the region. When I first moved to Portland in 1967, I immediately contacted the Portland Players, the city's largest community theater. Over the next two years I was cast in four roles, all nonpaying, which led to my meeting several people who were actively involved in the advertising industry. It wasn't too long before they were offering me employment in locally produced radio and television commercials.

What about children's theatre? Many children's theatres have moved away from the concept of children doing plays for children and toward the use of professional casts. If there is a professional children's theatre near you it is probably non-Equity and will draw its actors from the local community. While children's theatre is not the place for an actor to get rich, it *is* an excellent training ground. However, you should be warned that many children's theatres tour their shows, which might hamper some of your marketing efforts in the other actors' employment categories. If children's theatre sounds interesting, contact the artistic director and ask to be included in the next set of auditions.

Are there any small non-Equity professional theatres in your area? Often they are started by actors and directors who want an outlet for their creative energies they can control. Keep an eye out for their ads and posters and go see their plays. Introduce yourself and say you want to work. The money won't be much, in fact there may not be any at first, but it's a foot in the professional door.

Working in Professional Theatre

Whereas the amateur theatre must work around its volunteers for rehearsal time, the professional theatre sets its own schedules and demands that actors follow them. Generally a professional theatre will rehearse a full-length, two- or three-act play in three to four weeks of all-day rehearsals, five or six days a week—depending on budget. Sometimes that rehearsal time will be only two weeks, or even less. Here the director reigns supreme, but the actor must know his or her craft.

Directors are not educators and don't have time to teach actors how to read lines or how to move about the stage. Rather, they will devote their energies to character analysis and exploration out of which collaborative decisions on playing techniques will be made. Although you might expect a dictatorial director in professional theatre, this is not always the case. Many professional directors allow actors lots of room to connect with their characters before they step in and dictate; expect to work creatively.

If, however, you don't bring your character to life in a reasonable amount of time, the director is under no obligation to keep you in the role. This is professional theatre after all; you're being paid, and you can get fired.

Although the process of putting a play together and performing it for the public is universal, audience expectations do vary.

Without taking anything away from amateur theatre's goal of reaching theatrical perfection, a college or community theatre audience might expect an occasional mishap to occur during the run of a play. Lines can be dropped, lighting cues and entrances missed, and sound cues flubbed. Of course these problems can occur in professional theatre too, but they are rarely tolerated by viewers. If they recur repeatedly, audiences will drift away.

The professional actor needs the discipline to work toward a performance goal of nothing less than perfect. It also takes great discipline to be consistent in performance night after night after night.

When cast in any theatrical role, work hard. Establish a

reputation of punctuality and dependability. Be flexible with directors so you're considered easy to work with. And don't let a bad review stop you from trying out for the next production. All actors worth their salt have been panned a few times. It goes with the territory.

Certainly it would be foolhardy to expect success in professional theatre without serious onstage and/or classroom training. Therefore, let me restate the position taken in Chapter 1 of this book: active involvement in educational and community theatre, to include intensive course work, may be necessary for you to fully prepare for this end of the business. The strategy outlined in this chapter may not work for you otherwise.

Looking for Movie Work

There are always job opportunities when Hollywood chooses your location in which to shoot a film. And you won't have to worry about all the things big-city professional actors go through to land a film job. You're ready right now, with or without acting experience.

Although it may only happen once in a lifetime in your local area, it probably *will* happen at least once, because television shows, miniseries, and theatrical movies are almost always shot on location. And the filmmakers routinely hire local people as extras and, sometimes, though rarely, for speaking parts.

If you look beyond the local area and take a *regional* perspective, there are probably several projects going on each year that you as a career-oriented actor will want to tap.

Keep your eye on the want ads in your local paper. Casting people from a film or TV series will advertise for talent. Sometimes they'll use a local casting agency to do this. Also, check in regularly with your state's film commission. Most states now have one, and since they're legislatively appointed, you can find out where they are through your local state representative or through your local library. It's the job of the state film commission to lure members of the film industry to your state and make things easy for them once they get there. Therefore, the commission will know where and when films are being done near you.

The film's casting director will set up a time for local people to come in and interview. You should arrive early unless you like waiting. This "interview" will probably be a "cattle call," where everyone shows up at the same time and will be seen on a first-come, first-served basis.

It is in this initial interview that you are screened for extra work and speaking parts. The casting people are looking for locals who fit their idea of local authenticity. They want a look or a quality that speaks to the reality of the location. For example, if a film about a Maine lobsterman is slated for a coastal Maine location, people in the lobstering community there are prime candidates for roles—even major ones. Why? Because it's tough to act and speak like a native Maine lobsterman unless you are one.

Therefore, let authenticity dictate what you wear and how you act at the interview. You'll have your best chance for a part—maybe even a speaking one—if you keep it simple and honest. Be yourself and wear something that speaks to the reality of the region. Casting people don't want to see business suits when they're looking for deer hunters in the West Virginia hills. If you choose the comfortable, casual clothes you normally wear, you'll be on the right track.

Don't worry about photographs, demo tapes, or résumés. Film people have come to your town looking for local color, not local actors. They want real people. If you are an actor, it might be wise to downplay that fact in this situation. If photographs are needed, the casting people will take Polaroids. Or, they'll videotape you.

Film directors often pride themselves on their unique abilities to get stunning performances out of people with no acting experience whatever. Your look and natural quality are what will get you a role when a movie comes to your town.

When it's your turn to interview, don't try to impress everyone with your acting ability. Just be yourself and relax. Nobody wants to work with pushy, nervous people. And don't expect to get rich doing extra work. You will be paid, yes, but the experience is what you're after.

If you're asked to read for a speaking role, try to read with spontaneity and believability. Read as conversationally as you can within the role's requirements. Don't "act." Be as real as you are with your friends.

Movie people expect locals to fall down with fear during the audition, so they'll try to help you relax. Maintain your composure, read naturally, and answer questions openly and honestly. Then you'll have a fighting chance.

Career-minded union and nonunion actors should get their headshots and résumés in the files of regional agents and casting agencies in order to be able to compete for speaking roles and extra parts cast through them. If the film is being produced under SAG jurisdiction, all the speaking roles will be under SAG contract and an agreed-on percentage of extra parts will be as well.

Sometimes a regional or local casting or modeling agency will be hired by the film's production company to handle all the casting chores.

To illustrate the importance of all this, consider two films recently shot in Maine. The first, *Bed and Breakfast*, under an agreement with the Screen Actors Guild, used well over a hundred local townspeople in Kennebunkport as paid extras during shooting—all of them nonunion. The second, *Graveyard Shift*, shot in Bangor, did the same; however, this film was even more fruitful for local actors because a few of them were given speaking parts under SAG contract. This immediately made them eligible to join SAG.

Except for the major roles, which were cast in Hollywood, both of these movies were cast locally by the Portland Models Group, Maine's largest modeling and talent agency.

Are you beginning to get the idea? It's relatively easy to be in a movie if you're willing to do extra work! And the possibility of a speaking part, admittedly rare unless you're a member of the unions, is nonetheless real, even for beginners.

Working in Movies

If you're cast as an extra, you'll be in the background of one or more scenes. You won't be allowed to make *eye* contact with the camera. Let's say, for example, that you are part of a crowd of shoppers in a scene shot in a department store. You'll be required to do what shoppers do, and you'll be told when and where to move by the director, working through his assistant director. The scene will be shot over and over again until everyone is satisfied that it's right.

These scenes can take a very long time to shoot, so be prepared for a long day. Overtime can be expected. When you're not working on the set, stay out of the way. Never try to chat with the stars, and never ask for a star's autograph. It's considered very bad form.

When playing a speaking role, expect the scene to be shot several times from at least three angles—a wide shot and close-ups of each character. Be flexible, and expect plenty of direction. The director will know if you lack experience and is well aware that the situation can be stressful. It's his job to help you relax and turn out a great performance.

Don't worry about how long it takes to shoot a scene. It will be shot as many times as it takes to satisfy the director.

WHAT TO CHARGE

Let the movie people tell you what they'll pay and accept it. They won't negotiate fees. This might be your first film and you'd probably do it for nothing, right? Well don't. You'll be offered some money, perhaps quite a bit. Take it and run.

STUDENT FILMS

One way to get valuable film acting experience is to offer your acting services to the many student filmmakers who are creating films at almost every university and college. These young filmmakers use locals and would-be actors, often giving them leading roles. Although you'll probably work for no pay, the education you'll receive will be worth it.

Check with the colleges near you for the names of student filmmakers and keep an eye on local newspapers for advertisements for actors for student films. You'll learn what goes into the making of a film—not just what's expected of actors, but the technical aspects as well. And you'll get a copy of your work that you can use to show your ability as you search for professional opportunities. Best of all, when you do get a chance to be in a television show, miniseries or movie, you won't feel like a novice.

Chapter

SEVEN

Commercial and Corporate Print

To begin, let's clearly differentiate between traditional "fashion" modeling and commercial and corporate "print."

The term *fashion modeling* implies that the model models something—usually clothes—in either runway or photographic situations. When one models clothes, he or she is called a fashion model. The concept of fashion modeling is often stretched to include many other types of products, where the sex appeal of the people displaying or shown using these products is an enticement for the public to buy. In both situations, exceptionally attractive faces and bodies are required to stimulate the fantasies of the viewer so he or she will *need* to buy. The model's *looks* help sell the product; in many cases, they command more attention than the product itself.

Fashion models with extraordinary looks gravitate to our major cities and earn tremendous incomes on those looks alone. Acting ability is not a requirement for these few, and they certainly don't need this book. And while fashion modeling may lead to a career in acting, it won't without acting ability and training. If you feel that fashion modeling is what you want to do, and you're not interested in becoming an actor, see Appendix B for books on how to start a modeling career.

Commercial and corporate print originates all over the

country and often relies more on acting ability and less on glamorous looks than does fashion modeling. Commercial and corporate print is thus better suited to those who want a well-rounded acting career that encompasses several related avenues of opportunity.

Commercial print includes thematic magazine, poster, billboard, and newspaper advertisements that sell products using average people in real or comic situations. Typical themes in or near your home town might include a housewife shopping, a husband banking, a couple buying a house, a family watching a burglar being attacked by a just-trained guard dog, a family enjoying a vacation, kids salivating over ice cream, a teenager enjoying an amusement park, or sweethearts dining in a restaurant. You get the picture. Many of these themes can be highly dramatic.

Corporate print includes business-oriented scenes for trade magazines, business magazines, trade newspapers, in-house brochures, advertising pamphlets, and the like. Typical situations show business men and women at their desks, at the photocopy machine, interacting socially, working at computers, in large and small meetings, in the elevator, or on the phone.

Commercial and corporate print work has the same parameters as commercial and corporate television. The idea is to know your type and play to it in headshots, composites, makeup, and wardrobe.

Projecting Personality

To be successful in commercial and corporate print you must be photogenic and project personality through the camera to the printed page. You'll need to be believable in your role, but you won't have words to help you. This is not always as easy as it sounds.

My wife occasionally appears in local television spots and thoroughly enjoys doing them. The one and only print job she had was a different matter entirely. It was for a trade magazine ad for supermarket refrigeration units, and her role fell under the category of "typical housewife."

The shoot was staged early in the morning at a new local

supermarket before the business day began. Her directions were simple: walk up and down the aisle pushing a shopping cart while selecting items from the refrigeration units, which were the focus of the ad.

Reaching for orange juice sounds easy, doesn't it? It wasn't! She had to angle her body and head to accommodate the camera, and she had difficulty grabbing the juice in a natural, everyday manner.

Forced to move and act unnaturally, she felt self-conscious before the still camera. She had difficulty making the situation real for herself and became stiff and inexpressive—exactly the opposite of the relaxed, happy housewife the ad's theme required. Sensitive to her problem, and knowing that my wife routinely shopped with at least two of our six kids, the photographer wisely brought a young child onto the set, and everything changed for the better. Now that she had another human being to relate to, my wife was able to live her photographic role in a more relaxed, natural manner.

This story illustrates the print actor's need to relate to inanimate objects with believable expressions and actions. A great deal of print work involves a lone actor working with—or without—products. The fact that the photographer could call up a child at a moment's notice during a location shoot is highly unusual. What if a child had not been found?

My wife decided she didn't want to continue with print work, because she had real difficulty working alone and holding expressive poses. She realized that it isn't professional to tell potential employers, I'm interested only in print work that involves other people. She continues to enjoy working in television commercials because she feels natural when speech, movement, and other people are involved.

Getting Ready
TESTING

Although the print actor uses many of the same skills as the film/video actor, still-photography work is different in some respects. Before you try to market yourself for print work, give it a try without putting your reputation on the line. *Testing* is the way to do it.

Testing means this: a photographer agrees to take your picture free of charge for the right to use the photos without paying you. In general the photographer hopes to use photos of you in his or her portfolio as a means of showing off photographic technique.

In most cases the photographer will want to try his own ideas, just as you'll want to try yours. If all goes well, you will both benefit. The photographer gets a model on whom to try new ideas; you get invaluable on-camera experience. So bring many changes of clothes to the testing session.

You and the photographer will be able to evaluate your (and the photographer's) work when the contact sheets are printed.

The best possible outcome of a testing session is for a photographer to have discovered a new talent, namely you. If your contact sheets show promise, the photographer may recommend you. Test with as many photographers as you possibly can. It's a way of developing opportunities.

A testing session often yields a workable headshot or a photograph that might work in a composite. If you're going to test for print, ask the photographer to shoot a few headshots as well as situation and character shots. If you get a good one, all it will cost you is the price of a print.

You might now think, I'm not sure I could just call a photographer and ask him to take my picture for nothing. Who would want to do that? The answer to that legitimate question is: almost any photographer, if you can be flexible about time.

The best way I know to approach photographers about testing is to visit their studios in person after requesting an appointment by phone. Don't be afraid to do this. Just pick up the phone and call them. Look in the yellow pages under commercial photographers and get busy. Tell them you're interested in testing—they'll know what you mean—and ask for an appointment so they can get a look at you.

One way to find out which photographers are most open to testing in your area is to ask the advice of a local or regional modeling agency, one that uses people for commercial and corporate print. Or ask the advice of some successful regional actors you've met. If they're successful, they're probably doing print and know many of the photographers in the region.

Most commercial photographers—at least the better ones—are very busy. You'd think the last thing they'd make time to do is take pictures of someone who wants to break into print. But the fact is that commercial photographers consider themselves artists, too. And they like nothing better than to shake off the print ads for a while to wallow in their art form. Usually they'll indulge this urge on weekends and evenings, and they'll need people as subjects at least some of the time. That's where you come in. The photographer has an angle too—practice, trying new techniques, and art for art's own sake.

HEADSHOTS AND COMPOSITES

Your commercial headshot will serve you well during the initial stages of seeking print work—especially on the local level. Since most of the work is actor- rather than fashion-oriented, a good, natural-looking headshot is all you need as you make the rounds.

After doing several print jobs, however, you might want to invest in the traditional model's composite—but with an actor thrust. A *composite* is a group of two or more photographs on one or more pages; it shows the model or actor in a variety of poses with a variety of looks. (*See Illustration 13.*)

While you certainly could start out with a composite, why go to the time and expense before you have to? Ad agencies and photographers in or near your home town—unless that happens to be in a major city—won't really need a composite to decide whether to hire you. If it's a good likeness, the headshot you use for commercials should provide a good idea about which roles might best suit you.

If you believe in doing everything in stages, however, your local print career will reach a point when a composite will say you're a seasoned professional. It pays to wait until you have several samples of actual work before you put the best

Illustration 13

All Ann Foskett's composite photos by Linda Holt.

An example of a typical actor/print composite.

of them together in a composite. Doing things this way tells people you've had some success already and you know what it's all about.

It is unproductive to invest in a quality composite before it can really work for you. If your headshot can do the job while you build credits and reputation, let it. Then spring for the composite when your momentum needs a boost.

Be judicious when deciding which photographs to include in your composite. You want it to reflect your photographic range.

No matter what *general* type you are, that type can be stretched in all directions based on the clothes you have on, the location in which you're photographed, and the expression you're projecting. If you are a "grandmother" type, your composite might show you with a young child in a warm home environment, as a bored cleaning lady, as an unhappy hospital patient, and as a little old lady in a funny-looking get-up. A "lawyer" type could be shown in a courtroom, as a jogger, in casual clothes with family, or as a corporate executive.

Just remember it's as essential to stay away from the cliché with a composite as it is with a headshot. Your expressions should be honest, and the photographs should look like you. Avoid seldom-called-for glamorous poses that say you're just showing off.

You should change your composite every couple of years or so, just as you should your commercial and corporate headshots, to reflect changes in you.

If you want to place real emphasis on corporate print, your composite must have at least one photo of you looking corporate or in a corporate setting, wearing appropriate dress. If you choose not to use a composite, you'll need a corporate-looking headshot in addition to your commercial headshot.

A corporate headshot should reveal your head and shoulders; your attire should be "all business." Your expression should be open, honest, and businesslike and should project authority. You needn't smile openly for this picture, but you should not appear unfriendly or hostile.

WARDROBE

A print professional needs a more extensive wardrobe than the actor who does only television commercials. Although your basic acting wardrobe will do for a while, once you commit to print you should slowly acquire working clothes for all seasons. Make certain that your wardrobe can stretch to fit the fringes of your type range.

You should remember that most actors and models have a greater type range in still photography than they do in film or television, because the frozen photograph depends heavily on clothing and background to show the viewer who and what you are.

Consider this example. In commercials, you are always cast as a doctor, a lawyer, or a businesswoman because you have a preppy, upscale look and *sound*. When you walk into auditions that's how *you* look; your personality reinforces this image because you've learned to play to your type. But couldn't you so alter your look that people would believe you as a blue-collar worker? The probability is good. If you just dress and comb your hair appropriately, carry a lunch pail, and work on an appropriate expression, you could become blue-collar for print. Therefore, your wardrobe might include one basic blue-collar outfit. Mine does. It's a pair of rugged work shoes, navy cotton twill work pants, a blue chambray work shirt, and a denim work jacket. Throw in a hard hat and I'm ready for the plant.

I also have lots of casual outfits on hand to fit a variety of situations to which I feel I can stretch. For example, while I don't look like a typical jock, my wardrobe can definitely help me look sporty. So when my print agent says be a golfer, I can look the part.

The point here is that you can and should be ready for anything. Blue-collar is a fringe type for me. I don't do it often, but I do it often enough to warrant owning an outfit. What are your fringe types? Think about it.

Always have plenty of wardrobe alternatives. Many print people get loads of work because they are reputed to have an extensive wardrobe range—costumes, if you will. A pool shot implies that you'll need to bring several bathing suits.

Most print actors build their wardrobes to include at least two, and more likely three or four, outfits for business, sports, casual, evening, vacation, and formal situations. Many also carry a selection of glasses to subtly alter their look. Obviously (unless money is no object) this kind of wardrobe will take a while to assemble. The best way to get started is to hold off buying anything other than your basic wardrobe until hired. Then buy for each job as it arises. After a while you'll have an extensive wardrobe.

MAKEUP

The camera doesn't lie. It's almost impossible to conceal heavy makeup in still photography; so unless you're asked to alter your face to take on a special character or age, keep makeup to a minimum.

Women should consult a professional cosmetologist and then purchase high-quality street makeup that complements their skin type and tone. Remember to go for a natural, not a glamorous effect. If glamor is required, there will no doubt be a makeup professional on hand to ensure you project the desired effect.

Men need little more than a stick of foundation to conceal blemishes as well as powder to remove shine and provide an even skin tone. In many situations translucent powder does the job for both men and women; you should always have some on hand.

Hairstyle for commercial and corporate print should always be middle of the road, just as it must for television commercials. This simply means it should be nondistracting, and shouldn't draw attention to itself. If a trendy, glamorous, or outrageous hairstyle is required for the shot, you'll be told in advance and a hairstylist will be there to work with you.

Your teeth *must* be well taken care of, so see your dentist for cleaning at least twice a year. (But if you're smart, you probably do that anyway!)

Hand (and Foot) Modeling

Are you blessed with perfect hands or feet? You're lucky if you are, because hand and foot models who hold or relate to products on television commercials and in print advertisements really clean up. Hand and foot models need only perfect hands and feet (the rest of them isn't seen), and they work all the time. Better still, they are paid the same hourly rate as other actors and models.

Obviously, hand and foot people don't need a headshot. They do need a composite showing their photogenic extremities holding or relating to various products shot from several angles. Foot models need feet that are the right size: women, size 6, men, size 8. Hand models are not restricted by size limitations.

These models must protect their feet or hands against all hazards and must maintain them in camera-ready condition at all times. This means no washing dishes or running around barefoot and lots of manicures.

Looking for Print Work

ON YOUR OWN

Going it alone in small-town print is easier than going solo in big cities. If there isn't an agent on hand to do the work for you, look for print work exactly as you looked for commercial work. Meet likely employers and show your potential.

You'll need to meet the art directors in ad agencies and ad directors in corporations and businesses. You'll also need to know free-lance commercial and corporate photographers and photographers who work for the audiovisual departments of businesses and corporations.

After phoning for appointments, bring your headshot, résumé, and composites with you and maintain a professional demeanor. If your looks are marketable, work for the minimum rates in your area (ask successful print actors what they are) until you're established. (For a detailed explanation of how to contact people for the first time by phone, see pages 34–38.)

WITH AN AGENT

Most small or midsize cities in this country have a modeling agency or two (often they are the same agents who work with local actors on radio and TV spots and sometimes films), and these agencies lock up 90 percent or more of the local print work. Why? Because they are tenacious as a breed and know how to fight for the people they represent.

A good agent knows all the local photographers and art directors by their first name and touches base frequently. Those same photographers and art directors rely on agents to save them time. They leave the leg work to the agents and often bypass unrepresented free lances.

Although you can circumvent the modeling agent, your chances of getting work are better with representation. The smart thing to do is meet your local agent or agents and try to sign with one.

This is the big question: HOW DO I GET AN AGENT? You'll need photographs and contact sheets from your testing sessions as well as your acting headshot and résumé to make your pitch. If the agent feels that you are photogenic and can act, you're in. Actors who can deliver a wide range of honest facial expressions are in demand, and there's always room for a fresh face.

To reiterate briefly the procedure for making initial contact with agents: first, discover who they are by using the yellow pages and asking the advice of experienced actors in your area; second, get them on the phone; and third, explain that you are a new actor in the marketplace and request an appointment. If you are denied an initial appointment you will probably be asked to submit your portfolio (at this point that's probably only your headshot and contact sheets) by mail for evaluation. If the agent is interested in you further, you'll be called.

Agents offer another benefit you will appreciate—they negotiate your fees. You will be given an hourly and a daily rate that are as high as the traffic will bear. No more haggling or setting a price on your work. The agent does it all and traditionally receives 10 percent of your fee from you and an additional 20 or 25 percent from your employer. In general, the employer pays the agent, who then pays you.

Don't expect to be paid quickly for print work. Whereas SAG and AFTRA require that their members be paid within twelve working days of any work performed, there are no such payment requirements in the print world. Sixty to ninety days same as cash is more like it.

Signing with the print agent means that you agree to work through that agency exclusively and will not free-lance, but it does not mean that you can stop marketing yourself.

GO-SEES

When your agent gets a call for a job that requires your type, you'll be asked to "go see" the art director or whoever is responsible for casting. You'll be expected to take a portfolio of photographs with you to demonstrate your photogenic qualities. You will be hired based on your portfolio and how you look at the go-see. So dress the part: If you have a good agent, you'll have go-sees all the time. Although you'll grow to hate them, they are part of paying your dues.

THE PORTFOLIO

Your portfolio, or *book* as models call it, should be neat and professional. In the fickle world of advertising and corporate print, packaging is much more than half the game.

Although it certainly won't hurt to be perceived as a pleasant person to have around, your *look* for the photograph in question is much more important. This is why your portfolio should contain your headshot, your composite (if and when you have one), and prints from testing and actual work assignments. Be sure your portfolio demonstrates your *range* of expressions and type and that you keep it up to date with your latest work.

DOING THE ROUNDS

When you're not on go-sees or working, your agent expects you to "make rounds." This means you visit photographers to show them your portfolio in the hope they'll recommend you to the agencies they commonly work for. This is a traditional, time-honored practice, and you'll have little trouble meeting with photographers as long as you're flexible about time. Always call first.

Photographers want to see actors for several reasons. First, they need lots of people to photograph—a stable; and second, they want to see what other photographers are doing. Just as an actor can learn tricks of the trade by watching television and plays, a photographer learns from the photographs of others.

The Print Shoot

Like the commercial shoot, you'll show up at an appointed time. In print this is usually about a half hour before the picture taking is set to begin. This initial half hour is for choosing wardrobe and freshening makeup. Always have your makeup with you; men should also bring shaving gear.

People involved in the shoot usually include at least the photographer (and an assistant, if any) and the art director or director of advertising. There may also be several others on hand—probably agency people and clients.

Start your hourly rate clock when you step before the camera and remember that since you're being paid by the hour, once the clock starts you are expected to work. The professional sees to necessities before the shoot starts and does not ask for breaks. If someone asks if you want a break, fine. Take one if you feel you need it.

Polaroids are often taken and analyzed for lighting before the photographer shoots on film. This process may take quite a while, so you should expect to wait on the set. Stay alert; photographers don't like to waste time once they've made up their minds to shoot. He or she will say, Here we go, this is for real. And the strobes will flash.

Usually the photographer will tell you exactly what to do. All you'll have to do is follow his instructions. It's that easy.

Don't be surprised if the print session goes very quickly once the lighting is set. With today's advanced equipment a great deal of film can be shot in a very short time. That's why most print jobs last only an hour or two. But that hour or two can pay off handsomely at today's rates. In general, the shot is taken many different ways to offer the client a wide choice. Nobody likes to repeat a shoot.

It's not unusual for a photographer to just bid you good-bye after a shoot without commenting on or complimenting your work. Don't let this bother you. When something is wrong you'll hear about it.

When the shoot's over, you'll sign a release; the person responsible for payment will fill out a voucher with billing information for your agent, or for you if you don't have one. If the session runs a few minutes over, don't charge for the extra time. When the session runs more than fifteen minutes over, however, charge in half-hour increments. Thus, a one-hour-and-seventeen-minute session would be charged at one and a half hours.

Always ask for copies of the finished product at the end of the shoot. Get someone from the ad agency or wherever to commit to sending you one within a specified period of time. That way, when the time has expired you can telephone to request prints if you haven't received them. Be pleasant and courteous when you call.

Follow-Ups

The print actor should follow up every job, go-see, and photographer interview with a thank-you note. All you have to do is send a postcard photograph of yourself. Postcard photos can be ordered at very reasonable cost from the same company that printed your bulk headshots. Use a different headshot for your postcard for variety; it's to your advantage because it shows yet another view of you. Aside from being the right thing to do, thanking people by mail is smart. It's another good way of keeping your face before potential employers.

As with commercial acting, overexposure in your home town may become a problem if you get lots of work. If it does you'll have to move on or commute to another area in order to continue working.

Chapter

EIGHT

Radio and Television News, Weather, and Sports

While few of them admit it, radio and television news personalities *are* actors of a sort and use many of the same skills. The major differences between the commercial and corporate actor and the news personality are in job qualifications, job-search techniques, and working conditions.

If you want to do news, you're going to have to move to a fairly remote area (if you don't live in one already) to get started. And before you do that, you'll need a college degree.

A good major would, of course, be broadcast journalism, if it's available. Straight journalism is also good. If your school doesn't have any journalism courses, go for a broad liberal arts background with lots of performance-related course work such as public speaking and voice and diction. Take acting and communication courses, too. The idea is to build confidence and poise and to understand the communication process. But don't forget those all-important political science, economics, history, geography, government, philosophy, religion, and sociology courses that will help you understand the world in which we live.

The news industry needs knowledgeable people who read the paper every day and can put current events into historical perspective. They must be able to think critically and write coherently.

Radio

The small—one- and two-station—markets still hire inexperienced people, because they don't offer high-enough salaries to attract experienced broadcasters. Those who start there can move up—but not without putting in at least a couple of years at low pay with terrible hours and plenty of hard work.

You can't just put in your time and two years later emerge as an "experienced" news reporter. You'll have to learn something while you're there—how to write for broadcast, how to think like a reporter, how to develop sources, and how to interview people. You'll have to read news copy with a sense of objective authority. When you're ready to move into a larger market, these skills will make or break you.

FINDING THAT FIRST JOB

Looking for that first job will be tough because there probably won't be any openings. Plenty of other would-be news personalities have already grabbed all the available positions and are now trying to scramble up the ladder. So what do you do? How do you get past this seemingly impossible barrier? You become a *stringer.*

Very small market stations that are serious about news and public service hire stringers to cover some of the local area because they usually only have one, or at the most two, full-time news people. They can't be everywhere at once, so they'll use stringers to cover the stories they can't or don't want to report themselves.

To get your foot in the door of a given station, first check to see whether they use stringers and whether they pay them. If they do, they probably also have some written information regarding format that you can use in formulating your stories. Then, find out what kinds of stories are *not* being reported and do them yourself on speculation. You do this by listening and using your common sense.

The station you want to crack probably beams its signal over a fairly wide geographical area that encompasses several towns. Is that station covering *all* the news and sports in its listening area? It's doubtful. What are they missing?

You'll find out by becoming very familiar with each town's government leaders, local issues, and sports teams. You'll go to what you believe will be a newsworthy meeting or event armed with a tape recorder and microphone and get a story.

Maybe your first one will be something like "Town Council Rejects Sewer Proposal." You'll go to a town council meeting and interview a town councilor or two and a member of their opposition to present the news—that the sewer proposal was rejected—and also get some townspeople's reaction to the news.

You'll immediately—maybe in the lobby of the town council's chambers if you're too far from home—take your recorded quotes and write a story that fits a maximum sixty-second format. Then you'll phone it or take it in to the station's news director and say: Here, take it. It's yours. Free. If you like it, let me string for you regularly. *If* they take it and *if* they like it they might ask you to continue stringing and let you use the station's resources for further reports.

Your worth as a stringer will be evaluated not only by the quality of the news you provide, but also by its timeliness. News directors are not interested in old news. That's why it's essential to get your stories written and submitted as soon as possible. If you ask a news director when he or she wants a story, you'll usually be told, I want it yesterday!

While you certainly won't make much money as a stringer, you will be paid for each story, usually a flat fee plus expenses. You'll also be given the equipment to bring back stories with "actuality."

Actuality is what most people call *sound bites*. It's the sound of the people involved in the story talking—the high school coach complaining about poor officiating or the head of the local environmental group praising the town's cleanup efforts. You may also want to do a *voicer*, which is simply the story done (voiced) by you at the scene.

Voicers are sometimes called ROSRS, or Radio On-Scene Reports, where you voice the story over background noise. Often you will do a wrap, which is a report done either in the studio or at the scene with your part on tape but including a piece of actuality. (*See Illustration 14.*)

At most stations these kinds of reports must be under sixty

Illustration 14

```
REPORTER:     GOVERNOR SMITH ANNOUNCED TODAY THAT STATE
              REVENUE FIGURES ARE RUNNING BELOW EXPECTATIONS.
              THE GOVERNOR SAYS IF THIS TREND CONTINUES HE'LL
              ASK THE LEGISLATURE TO TAKE ACTION.


ACTUALITY:    "IT MAY BE NECESSARY TO CUT SOME SERVICES, LAY
              OFF SOME STATE EMPLOYEES, OR, AS A LAST
              RESORT, RAISE TAXES.  I HOPE NOT, BUT WE'VE GOT
              TO BE PREPARED IF THE ECONOMY DOESN'T IMPROVE."


REPORTER:     SO FAR THIS FISCAL YEAR THE STATE HAS COLLECTED
              ABOUT TEN MILLION DOLLARS LESS THAN CALLED FOR
              IN THE SMITH ADMINISTRATION'S BUDGET.  AT THE
              STATEHOUSE, I'M JOE REPORTER FOR WXXX NEWS.
```

A typical news wrap with actuality.

seconds. So you have to be able to write concisely and know how to edit audiotape. When you start to bring actuality tapes back to the studio to edit them down, ask someone there to show you the ropes. It's easy.

You'll probably have five minutes of interview on tape for every ten seconds you'll use in the story. You'll learn how to skim through a tape to find the newsworthy statements in no time, and assembling your final report will quickly become second nature.

The more you string for a station the closer you will be to a full-time position, particularly if you make yourself indispensable by working extra hard and covering lots of events. You should try to get something on the radio every morning during *drive time*—when people are driving to work in their cars. Morning drive time is prime time in radio, and it's when the most people will be listening to you.

The important thing when you're trying to get a radio news job is to get lots of voicers and wraps on the air so that people hear your voice. (If all you do is get actuality, how does anyone know who's getting it?) And make sure your reports are well written. After a while the station's general manager may say: I hear this person every day. She's doing a great job for us.

When the general manager knows who you are and thinks you're a hard-working go-getter who can write, you're in a good position to land that first full-time job. Your opportunity comes when a person on the news staff moves on to a bigger market.

At that point let the general manager, or news director if the station has one, know that you want the job badly and will put up with lousy working conditions to get it. Offer to work a split shift, to work mornings and evenings and cover meetings in between. Enthusiasm means a great deal at this level.

I know this sounds like you're being asked to offer the news director the moon. You are. And you better be damn sure you can deliver or you'll never survive in this business.

MOVING UP

Once you get into a full-time job in a small-market radio station, you may be able to move up from there. While there are way too many applicants for those medium- and large-market jobs, there are way too few with really good experience.

What is good experience? Staying on that first job for at least two years while developing professional reporting skills under difficult conditions. The theory is that if you can overcome the limitations of the small markets and turn out quality work, you'll do okay when you get to a larger market with lots more news to report.

So put in a major effort during that first job. You should approach every assignment—even the lost-cat-and-dog stories—as though it were an important one. The people you report on now won't forget you as they move up in their professions: if you treat them honestly today, they'll be good news sources for you tomorrow.

You can make major strides toward a job in a larger market by stringing for big stations on stories that happen in your area. If something's coming up that's major—statewide or regional—call the large stations and ask whether you can cover the story for them. Go with the first station in each bigger market that agrees to let you string the story and forget the rest. Since a radio market covers a specific population area, you can string for more than one large station as long as they do not compete in the same market for the same listeners. (This means that if you live in a midsize city such as Boise, Idaho, you can only string for one radio station that broadcasts in greater Boise.)

Worm into as many radio markets as you can, and do your stories cheap. If you're looking for a job, don't try to squeeze as much money as you possibly can out of these stations. If they like your work, they'll come back to you and you can charge more then. So watch for news events of greater-than-local interest, such as murder trials, and offer to pass them on. Do it regularly and do it well.

Stringing for a large station is the same as stringing for a smaller one. After a while you become a presence, and you have an advantage when a job opens up.

Does all this sound like a tall order? It is. Holding down a full-time radio news job and stringing for bigger stations at the same time puts you through your paces. But that's how it's done. After you've worked for a while you should have enough for a quality demo tape and an impressive résumé to help you move up.

Do your marketing systematically. Look around the immediate area. Where are the news stations in your state? Where are the bigger towns and cities? Look for two-, three-, and four-person news staffs and make sure they all receive a *current* tape and résumé. If your tape is more than six months old, make and send a new one.

Make sure that tape is perfect. There should be no technical glitches; it should present a good overall view of what you can do; and it should be relatively short. Contents might include one full newscast and a feature story you've done—all in ten minutes or less. Put this on a cassette tape with a neatly typed label containing your name, address, and phone number.

Your résumé should be flawless. If there are typos or misspellings, forget it. It'll go in the trash. (This is no exaggeration!) Your résumé should show what you can do. Don't pad it with extraneous fluff. It should, however, contain any radio-related experience, even if it wasn't paid. (*See Illustration 15.*)

Your demo tape and résumé should be sent out under a cover letter that is coherently written. You're asking for a news job. And sloppiness, misspellings, or poor writing will knock you out of the race before the starting pistol fires.

When you get an interview at a medium- to large-market station, stay low-key and stress your professionalism in terms of work ethic. If you have experience at a small-market station only, you'll be viewed as still having plenty to learn. So don't puff yourself up to something you're not. Be yourself and be honest about your weaknesses as well as your strengths.

Television News

With the right educational background and the right looks and voice, television news may the next area for you to consider. While there's no guarantee that you can make the move easily, radio news has always been a good conduit to

Illustration 15

```
                    RESUME

               Julie A. Flowers
                 P.O Box 111,
                Smalltown, USA
                    00000

             Tel.:  (208)555-6665
```

Objective:
To seek employment as a news reporter in radio broadcasting, with duties which include regular news beats and an anchoring position.

Experience:
October, 1988 - September, 1989. Part-time news reporter for WRNR radio, Martinsburg, West Virginia.

Duties: Covered regular news beats, including the City Council, the Board of Education, the Court system, and the County Commission. During this tenure, I assumed the responsibilities for writing and anchoring 3 afternoon news broadcasts, 5 days per week. Also became the Public Service Director. These duties were all held concurrently.

September, 1989 - May, 1990. Promoted to: Assistant News Director (full-time) for WRNR radio, Martinsburg, West Virginia.

Duties: In addition to the duties described above, I assumed responsibilitiy for the production of all newscasts, and increased the news output by 6 additional broadcasts per day.

Related Experience:
October, 1988 - May, 1990. Regular contributor to the Charleston Bureau of the Associated Press and West Virginia Public Radio

Education:
Associate in Applied Science from Parkland College, Champaign, Illinois, majoring in Broadcast Performance and minoring in Journalism.

Personal Information:
Born, September 18, 1964, in Pontiac, Illinois. Married, husband is also a broadcast announcer and producer.

This is the résumé of a radio news broadcaster whose career is just getting under way. The format is simple and easy to read.

Charles S. Gilley
17 M Street
Somewhere, ME 04106
(207) 666-5556

PROFESSIONAL OBJECTIVE: Radio News, Production

PROFESSIONAL EXPERIENCE:

<u>News Director/Public Service Director,</u> WCLZ Brunswick, Maine
Supervised news and public service departments; Wrote and announced morning
news; Produced weekly public affairs interview program; Wrote and produced
recorded news features; Wrote and maintained live public service
announcements; Maintained public service files; Compiled, wrote, and published
quarterly issues and programs reports (1988-present)

<u>Announcer/Public Service Director,</u> WCLZ Brunswick, Maine
Announced news and music broadcasts for adult contemporary
formats; Wrote and maintained live public service announcements; Wrote and
produced advertisments (1985-1988)

<u>Announcer,</u> WMGX Portland, Maine
Announced music programs for rock format (1984-1985)

<u>Announcer,</u> WDEA-WWMJ Ellsworth, Maine
Announced news and music broadcasts for jazz and adult contemporary formats;
Produced advertisements (1983-1984)

<u>Account Executive,</u> Windjammer Communications Skowhegan, Maine
Sold radio advertising; Gained new clients; Wrote advertising copy (1983)

<u>Station Manager,</u> WMEB-FM Orono, Maine
Managed executive staff of ten people and a general staff of sixty people;
Performed all administrative tasks at WMEB (Music, programming, traffic, etc.);
Created and implemented $20,000 budget (1982-1983)

<u>Production Director,</u> WMEB-FM Orono, Maine
Managed production staff; Created promotional announcements for station
activities (1981-1982)

<u>Disc Jockey,</u> WMEB-FM (1980-1983)

<u>News Producer,</u> WMEB-FM (1980-1981)

EDUCATION:

B.A., University of Maine, Orono, Maine May 1983
Major: Broadcasting
Minor: International Affairs (German)

This résumé is similar in design but presents a bolder approach.

television news. In radio you'll have learned to meet dead-lines, get out and get stories, and work quickly. You'll have written for broadcast and have read broadcast copy.

You can also get into TV news by going to a good broad-cast journalism college that has the technical facilities to teach you what you need to know. You'll need a school that lets you practice reporting news rather than just talking about it—like Northwestern or the University of Missouri. The grad-uate school of broadcasting at Northwestern operates a per-manent news bureau in Washington. Students spend a semester there working as stringers for television and radio stations around the country. It's probably the best experience you can get for TV, and students there often walk into jobs. But getting into the program isn't easy. Missouri operates a network of affiliated stations in a competitive market.

Another way to break in is luck. There are stories of peo-ple who were in the right place at the right time who got an on-camera TV news job with no experience at all. But those stories are few and mostly old. Experience is essential today because the news business takes itself very, very seriously.

To get into TV news from either radio or college, you'll probably have to start in a very small market—just as in ra-dio. There are 215 market areas in this country, based on population density. The further down you get in market number, the greater the odds that someone will take a chance and hire you.

Because the competition is intense for almost *all* TV news jobs, no matter the market, the key is to get your foot in the door somewhere and then move up using your experience to help sell you.

Breaking in at the bottom isn't easy either. Even in the smallest markets, news directors want to see tape. This means you have to have access to three-quarter inch—not VHS as in home video—tape facilities, or you'll have a problem.

A friend in the business might help you, or you might use the facilities of a local college. Alternatively, you can buy the services of a production studio. Whichever way you go, your tape must contain some field reporting. It's not enough to sit in a news set and read a story from a teleprompter à la Dan Rather.

Many television stations will understand your inability to put together a truly professional demo tape and may give you a screen test—but only if you have the qualities they're looking for. Over and above your education and radio news experience, TV stations want people with brains who aren't afraid of hard work.

Once you've contacted a news director and are invited in for an interview, don't say you want to be a TV star. You won't get a job. Rely on the fact that you're aware of what goes on in the world, that you read the paper every day, and that you know what goes on in your community. You can say *this* to a news director.

The news director doesn't just want you to smile and look good: that's the least of it. You can learn that part of the job. What can't be taught is an air of authority and an ability to analyze issues while you provide perspective for the viewer.

If your aim is to sit in an anchor's chair, aim somewhere else, at least for a while. It's difficult to become an anchor without some reporting experience, which requires more than a pretty face and a pleasing voice.

When you get to the anchor's chair your image and authority will take over from your reporting skills. Although you'll undoubtedly be asked to *write* news, most of your duties will revolve around your ability to *present* news.

Television Weather

There is more room for theatre and personality in weather than in news.

Some TV stations, the ones with the most money, search for the person who combines knowledge of meteorology with on-air talent. Smaller stations usually look for one or the other, with emphasis on personality.

That's where you might come in. You'll find a few small-market stations that won't care if you know weather, because they have access to weather information. (A degree in meteorology is nevertheless a definite asset in any market.)

They just want someone who will project a personality and deliver the weather report with a sense of knowledge and authority. This means you'll have to do some reading to understand what those tightly packed isobars (or lines of even pressure) mean (windy, very windy).

In the old days knowledge of weather almost always took a back seat to entertainment. That's why weathermen (yes, weather*men*) were often asked to present their reports comically. This was done for years. Then women got in on the act and sold sensuality along with balmy days. Today it's more serious. But you still need spark to brighten up all that meteorologic monotony.

If you want to break into television with no background at all, weather reporting at a small station might just be your ticket. If you look right and can project a pleasing, spunky personality, you might have a chance. Try it and see.

Make a demo tape of a mock weather forecast using whatever facilities you can—the more professional the better. Then take it around. The next time a weather slot opens up, maybe you'll get the nod.

Once you're working you can try to ease into news reporting. It may not be easy, but many a network news personality has had a stint doing the weather.

Television Sports

Sports reporting also has some room for personality and theatricality; but unlike weather, you gotta know sports. Well, at least you gotta look and act like you know sports.

The television sports audience won't stand for someone who doesn't project real enthusiasm for and understanding of sports in general. If you don't have these qualities, forget it. You won't be able to fake it night after night, so don't even try.

If you do want to do sports and believe you have the requisite qualifications, it's a great area because TV stations often encourage creativity to pull in viewers. Watch the local network and cable sports shows in your area for a few nights to see the variety of presentations. Then put together a creative demo tape.

It's okay to copy others' formats, but your tape should show that *you* can be different. This is where your personality comes in. How do *you* analyze a local team's success? How do *you* feel about a highly paid player's holdout?

If the news director thinks your personality will appeal to a good percentage of those sports fans out there, he'll take a chance on you even if you don't have much on-air experience.

Conflicts of Interest

Those news personalities who want to use their notoriety to land lucrative corporate spokesperson jobs may find the going rough. Station managers usually nix the idea because of the perceived conflict of interest.

The theory is that if you're working for a corporation, then you cannot objectively report about that corporation. The same is true with commercials. You will almost never see news personalities doing commercials, although they often do public service announcements when the message doesn't represent a conflict.

If you're thinking about using radio and television news, sports, and weather as a springboard to an acting career, remember that you won't be able to do both at the same time.

Appendix

The Major Actors' Unions

The American Federation of Television and Radio Artists

AFTRA comprises television and radio broadcasters (news, weather, sports, interviewers, disc jockeys, and other on-air personnel), videotaped programs (as opposed to filmed programs), videotaped corporate/industrial programs, videotaped commercials, and radio commercials.

Here's the good news. AFTRA has *open membership.* This means that, at this writing, anyone who can afford to plunk down the initiation fee can join. You should note, however, that there is a move on to combine AFTRA with the Screen Actors Guild (SAG), which has restrictions on membership.

At this time no one knows what that will mean, but it's probably a good bet that the new, merged union—if it *ever* comes—will have some restrictions on membership. Therefore, if you are thinking about union membership now, it might be to your advantage to join AFTRA before a union merger. It could be an easy ticket into SAG.

AFTRA LOCALS

To find the current phone number and address of the AF-TRA local nearest you, consult the yellow pages in the following cities:

Albany	Atlanta	Boston	Buffalo
Chicago	Cleveland	Dallas	Denver
Detroit	Fresno	Hawaii	Houston
Kansas City	Los Angeles	Miami	Nashville
New Orleans	New York	Omaha	Peoria
Philadelphia	Phoenix	Pittsburgh	Portland, OR
Rochester	Sacramento	San Diego	San Francisco
Schenectady	Seattle	St. Louis	Stamford, CT

Also look up the Tri-State local—which covers Cincinnati, Columbus, Dayton, Indianapolis, and Louisville—in the Cincinnati yellow pages; the Twin Cities local in the Minneapolis yellow pages; and the Washington/Baltimore local in the Bethesda, MD yellow pages.

When contacting these AFTRA regional offices, request a membership application form. Then mail it back with the appropriate initiation fee and initial dues payment. It's that easy.

BASIC AFTRA RULES

The basic AFTRA rules applicable in the commercial, recording, and industrial/educational markets are these:

1. AFTRA members may not agree to work for any producer who is not a signatory to the applicable AFTRA contract.
2. It is the member's responsibility to contact AFTRA to verify a producer's signatory status before accepting a job offer.
3. Members may not work for any producer against whom the Federation is conducting a strike, or violate any strike order of the Federation.

4. It is the members responsibility to report any violation of a Federation contract to AFTRA.

The Screen Actors Guild

Things get a little more complicated with SAG. This union covers filmed (as opposed to videotaped) television commercials, theatrical films, television films and shows, and industrial/corporate films. Its national headquarters is in Hollywood, California.

SAG has clear membership restrictions. In order to join SAG you must:

1. Have performed in a principal role (a principal is a performer with lines or special business that advances the story line), or
2. Have worked three days as an extra under SAG jurisdiction at SAG wages (an extra is background talent, used only in nonprincipal roles), or
3. Be a member of a sister union (Actors' Equity Association, AFTRA, AGVA [Variety Artists], AGMA [Musical Artists], or ACTRA [the Canadian actors' union]) for at least one year and have proof (a signed contract) of principal work under that union's jurisdiction.

REGIONAL SAG OFFICES

To request an application form, which will spell out the required initiation and dues payments, look up the phone number and address of the regional SAG office nearest you. A list of the branch offices follows:

Arizona (Phoenix)	Atlanta
Boston	Chicago
Cleveland	Dallas (Irving)
Denver	Detroit (Lathrup Village)
Florida (Miami)	Hawaii (Honolulu)
Houston	Minneapolis/St. Paul
Nashville	New York
Philadelphia	St. Louis

San Diego   San Francisco
Seattle   Washington, D.C. (Chevy
                         Chase, MD)

BASIC SAG RULES

1. SAG members may not agree to work for any producer who is not a signatory to the applicable SAG contract.
2. It is the member's responsibility to contact SAG to verify a producer's signatory status before accepting a job offer.
3. Members may not work for any producer against whom the Guild is conducting a strike, or violate any strike order of the Guild.
4. It is the members responsibility to report any violation of a Guild contract to SAG.

For additional information on SAG rules, contact your regional SAG office.

Actors' Equity Association

The AEA represents theatrical performers and stage managers in the legitimate theatre throughout the United States. There are three ways to gain membership in Equity:

1. Upon signing an Equity contract with a producer, or
2. By being a member of any of Equity's sister unions for a period of one year and having performed under the jurisdiction of that union—called the parent union—either as a principal performer or for three days of work comparable to an extra performer on a nonwaiver basis. The sister unions—the Four A's—are also known as the Associated Actors and Artists of America and consist of nine branches: AEA, AFTRA, AGMA (Musical Artists), AGVA (Variety Artists), SAG, SEG (Screen Extras Guild), APATE (Association Puertoriquena de Artistas y Technicos Del Espectaculo), IAU (Italian Actors Union), and HAU (Hebrew Actors Union), or

3. Through the Membership Candidate Program, which allows nonprofessional actors to credit their work at a participating theatre toward Equity membership.

JOINING EQUITY

For details on joining Equity and for an application form, call or write AEA at the national office at 165 West 46th Street, New York, NY 10036. AEA also maintains branch offices in Chicago, Los Angeles, and San Francisco.

BASIC EQUITY RULES

1. Members may not rehearse or perform in an Equity company without a properly signed contract.
2. Members must, upon signing an Equity contract, notify the Equity office and file the Equity copy of the contract with the Equity office.
3. Members are not permitted to perform with or stage manage a non-Equity company—with or without pay—without permission of Equity.

Check with the union office nearest you for additional rules.

Appendix

Recommended Practical Reading

For textbooks on acting, journalism, voice and diction, and other related subjects a leisurely browse through your closest university bookstore is suggested. The books recommended here are career and how-to oriented. They were chosen to help you broaden your practical knowledge of the professional acting field and to aid you in dealing with the realities of the national acting arena.

Acting Guides and Directories

Adams, Brian. *Screen Acting: How to Succeed in Motion Pictures*. Beverly Hills: Lone Eagle Publications, 1987.

Blum, Richard A. *Working Actors: The Craft of Television, Film, & Stage Performance*. Stoneham, MA: Focal Press, 1989.

Brandstein, Eve, and Joanna Lipari. *The Actor: A Practical Guide to a Professional Career*. New York: Donald I. Fine Inc., 1987.

Callan, K. *The New York Agent Book: How to Get the Agent You Need and the Career You Want*. Studio City, CA: Sweden Press, 1989.

———. *The L.A. Agent Book: How to Get the Agent You Need and The Career You Want*. Studio City, CA: Sweden Press, 1990.

Charles, Jill, ed. *Summer Theater Directory*. Dorset, VT: Theater Directories, 1990.

———, ed. *Regional Theatre Directory, 1990–91*. Dorset, VT: Theatre Directories, 1990.

———, ed. *Directory of Theatre Training Programs II*. Dorset, VT: Theatre Directories, 1990.

Charles, Jill, with Tom Bloom. *The Theatrical Picture/Resume Book*. Dorset, VT: Theatre Directories, 1991.

Cohen, Robert. *Acting Professionally: Raw Facts About Careers in Acting*. Mountain View, CA: Mayfield, 1989.

Fridell, Squire. *Acting in Television Commercials*. New York: Crown, 1987.

Henry, Mari L., and Lynne Rogers. *How to Be a Working Actor: The Insider's Guide to Finding Jobs in Theater, Film and Television*. New York: M. Evans & Company Inc., 1989.

Hines, Terrance, and Susy Vaughan. *An Actor Succeeds: Career Management for the Actor*. New York: Samuel French Inc., 1989.

Jenkins, Glo, and Barbara Britt. *Commercials: A Handbook for Performers*. Glassboro, NJ: Kronos, 1981.

Lewis, M.K., and Rosemary Lewis. *Your Film Acting Career: How to Break into the Movies & TV & Survive in Hollywood*. New York: Crown, 1983.

Moore, Dick. *Opportunities in Acting Careers*. Lincolnwood, IL: National Textbook Co., 1985.

Auditions

Black, David. *The Actor's Audition*. Westminster, MD: Random House, 1990.

Bluhm, Annika. *The Methuen Audition Book for Men*. Dist. by Heinemann Educational Books, Portsmouth, NH, 1989.

———. *The Methuen Audition Book for Women*. Dist. by Heinemann Educational Books, Portsmouth, NH, 1989.

Bollow, Ludmilla. *One Acts and Monologues for Women*. New York: Broadway Play Publishing Inc., 1983.

Bolton, Martha. *Humorous Monologues.* New York: Sterling Publishing Co., Inc., 1989.

Earley, Michael, and Philippa Keil, eds. *Solo: The Best Monologues of the 80's.* New York: Applause Books, 1987.

Ellis, Roger. *Audition Handbook for Student Actors.* Chicago: Nelson-Hall, 1985.

Friedman, Ginger. *The Perfect Monologue.* New York: Bantam, 1990.

Karshner, Roger. *Monologues They Haven't Heard.* Toluca Lake, CA: Dramaline Publications, 1990.

Shurtleff, Michael. *Audition.* New York: Walker & Co., 1984.

Smith, Marisa, and Kristin Graham, eds. *Monologues From Literature: A Sourcebook for Actors.* New York: Fawcett Columbine, 1990.

Voice

Eisenson, Jon. *Voice and Diction.* New York: Macmillan, 1985.

Keith, Michael C. *Broadcast Voice Performance.* Stoneham, MA: Focal Press, 1988.

Utterback, Ann. *Broadcast Voice Handbook, How to Polish Your On-Air Delivery.* Chicago: Bonus Books, 1990.

Broadcast Journalism

Hough, George A. *News Writing.* Boston: Houghton Mifflin, 1988.

Pearleman, Donn. *Breaking Into Broadcasting.* Chicago: Bonus Books, 1986.

Swann, Phil, and Ed Achorn. *How to Land a Job in Journalism.* White Hall, VA: Betterway Publications, 1988.

Teel, Leonard R., and Ron Taylor. *Into the Newsroom: An Introduction to Journalism.* Chester, CT: Globe Pequot, 1988.

White, Ray. *Building a Career in Broadcast Journalism.* Stoneham, MA: Focal Press, 1989.

Modeling

Anderson, Marie. *Model: A Complete Guide to Becoming a Professional Model.* New York: Doubleday, 1989.

Gearhart, Susan W. *Opportunities in Modeling.* Lincolnwood, IL: National Textbook Co., 1987.

Goldman, Larry. *Becoming a Professional Model.* New York: Morrow, 1986.

Appendix

*How to Get
a Wireless Earprompter*

There are three companies that currently manufacture wireless earprompters, although they may not call them that. The technical jargon goes this way: it's a "telcoil only" unit that has no environmental microphone to receive external signals. It only receives induction signals through a neck loop.

When you call or write them seeking the names and addresses of authorized representatives in your area, you'll have to use language they can understand. So ask them where you can get a "telcoil only" ear device in your area, then go to the representative and bring this book with you. If they haven't fitted anyone for an earprompter before, the illustrations and text found here should provide all the information *they'll* need to give you what *you* need.

All three of these companies make custom (this means molded to *your* ear canal) earprompters. Two of them make their units with an intensity wheel, which allows you to vary the intensity of the sound you hear through the unit. Although the cost of units with this feature is greater, the flexibility you get is worth it.

The companies, all of which sell their product through authorized representatives only, are:

1. OTICON, 29 Schoolhouse Road, Somerset, New Jersey 08873. Telephone: (800) 526–3921. Oticon makes a custom earprompter with an intensity wheel.
2. STARKEY, 6700 Washington Avenue South, Eden Prairie, Minnesota 55440. Telephone: (800) 328–8602. Starkey makes a custom earprompter with no intensity wheel.
3. COMTEK, 357 West 2700 South, Salt Lake City, Utah 84115. Telephone: (801) 466–3463. Comtek makes a custom earprompter with an intensity wheel. They also manufacture a generic (one size fits all) earprompter with an intensity wheel for less cost.

Prices for these units vary. At this writing all of them can be purchased for under $400.00. But you know how these things go. Mostly up.